The CHICKEN

Race Point
PUBLISHING

A division of Book Sales, Inc.
276 Fifth Avenue, Suite 206
New York, New York 10001

RACE POINT PUBLISHING and the distinctive
Race Point Publishing logo are trademarks of Book
Sales, Inc.

This 2012 edition published by Race Point
Publishing by arrangement with
Ivy Press, 210 High Street, Lewes,
East Sussex, BN7 2NS, UK

Creative Director Peter Bridgewater
Art Director Wayne Blades
Project Editor Judith Chamberlain-Webber
Designer Andrew Milne
Photographer Andrew Perris
Picture Researcher Katie Greenwood

ISBN-13: 978-1-937994-03-7
Color origination by Ivy Press Reprographics
Printed in China

2 4 6 8 10 9 7 5 3 1

www.racepointpub.com

The CHICKEN
A Natural History

DR JOSEPH BARBER WITH JANET DALY,
CATRIN RUTLAND, DR MARK HAUBER
& ANDY CAWTHRAY

Race Point
PUBLISHING

Contents

Introducing the Chicken

The chickens of today are descended from the jungle fowl of Southeast Asia. The process of domestication probably began almost 10,000 years ago, when humans started to take pleasure in the bloodthirsty spectacle of cockfighting. Champion fighters were no doubt encouraged to stay close to the human settlement—along with the groups of hens that naturally accompanied them.

For these early chickens, this arrangement would have worked to their advantage; they would have been afforded some protection against their natural predators, and given access to food scraps, grain, and the assorted invertebrates that live in and around a settlement. And, as social birds, they would have been likely to respond well to their new-found "keepers," all the while becoming better adapted to the human environment with each generation.

Our ancestors, too, must have gradually come to notice how efficiently chickens converted their food sources into eggs and meat. Over time, chickens, therefore, became part of the scenery and, indeed, part of the culture—with evidence suggesting that they soon became used for spiritual and medicinal purposes. Over the next few thousand years, humans began to congregate in ever greater numbers in established locations, and chickens would probably have been found living closely among them.

By and large, they were seen simply as a handy but casual source of meat and eggs, with only the ancient Romans (in typically enterprising fashion) applying any kind of industrialized approach to rearing them as a food source. However, true industrialized chicken farming—and breeding—would not begin until the middle of the twentieth century.

Right *Chickens have been part of the lives of humans for thousands of years.*

A REWARDING SPECIES

With the advent of industrialized farming, the relationship between humans and chickens has changed, but the idea of the backyard chicken still has its attractions. Some people keep fowl for the same reason that others enjoy growing flowers and vegetables in their garden—for the simple pleasure of seeing modest reward for honest toil. And when it comes to the yard, chickens are only too happy to provide extra benefits; they peck away at common pests, such as ticks, ants, caterpillars, snails, and slugs (and the occasional prized cabbage or lettuce—no-one said they were perfect), and they also provide an organic, high-nitrogen fertilizer on a daily, often hourly, basis, which is well worth adding to your compost or mulch.

Almost all owners enjoy cooking and eating freshly harvested chicken eggs. This is not just because they taste better than intensively farmed alternatives—although they really do—but because there is a satisfaction in knowing just where your food has come from. This stands in stark contrast to the guilt people often feel after eating cheaper chicken or eggs from intensive farming systems, where poor welfare and suffering can be commonplace. In an age where we have become geographically and psychologically distanced from our food, there is something to be said for locally grown produce—and you cannot get more local than your own backyard.

Other keepers of chickens revel in the everyday interaction with another species, as people do with other kinds of pet or livestock. Chickens are undeniably rewarding company: they recognize and respond to their keepers; they indulge in all kinds of fascinating behavior; and they bring color and movement to your backyard. They also serve to teach children about the cycle of life, and about the effort and responsibility required to get food from the land.

ABOUT THIS BOOK

This book is for anyone interested in chickens, whether you keep some already or whether you are thinking about it. It treats chickens not simply as producers of meat and eggs but as fascinating creatures in their own right. In the first four chapters, you will discover all that science can tell us about the origins, anatomy, behavior, and capabilities of modern domesticated chickens. And in the fifth, you will find an introduction to the many breeds of chicken that exist in all their richness and variety. By the time you finish this book, you will be able to understand a great deal more about how these amazing birds live and how you can help them thrive. Welcome to the world of chickens.

10 FASCINATING FOWL FACTS

1. Chickens are descended from dinosaurs.

2. Chickens outnumber humans by almost three to one. Around 19 billion are reared worldwide every year.

3. Chickens are the most populous bird species alive.

4. In 2010, there were more than 1,400 breeds of chicken but a total of forty three breeds were considered extinct.

5. Hens lay eggs even without a male; some breeds can lay up to 260 eggs per year, with some individuals able to lay over 300.

6. Hens prefer to mate with dominant males; they can eject the sperm of more subordinate males after copulation.

7. Chicks "cheep" to each other while still within their eggs, which can result in them hatching at the same time.

8. Chickens can run as fast as nine miles per hour.

9. Chickens have a good sense of smell—chicks can even react to odors they were exposed to before hatching.

10. Chickens naturally live to between five and ten years of age, and some can reach fifteen to sixteen. In commercial settings with access to nutritional food, broiler chickens reach slaughter weight at just five to six weeks of age.

KEY CHICKEN TERMS

Bantam A small or miniature breed of chicken. Many large breeds of domestic chickens have miniature counterparts that are also termed bantam varieties.

Broiler Chicken breeds selected for fast growth, large appetites, higher muscle mass, and a greater efficiency for converting feed into weight gain.

Capon A castrated male chicken.

Chick A baby chicken.

Cock British term for a mature male chicken—known as a rooster in the United States and Canada.

Cockerel Often used to describe an immature male chicken, a male less than one year of age, or a male of any age.

Hen A female chicken that lays eggs (egg laying can begin at about 20 weeks of age).

Layer Chicken breeds selected for frequent egg laying, not for their meat, with some breeds able to lay more than 250 eggs per year.

Pullet A female chicken not yet mature enough to lay eggs, or commonly less than a year old.

Rooster A mature male chicken—known as a cock in the UK.

CHAPTER 1

Evolution & Domestication

Origins of the Domestic Chicken

The earliest evidence of domesticated chickens (*Gallus domesticus*) has been found at various sites throughout China dating back to around 5400 BCE. This is later than the dog (the earliest animal to be domesticated), cat, sheep, pig, goat, and cow, but earlier than the horse or donkey.

ANCIENT ANCESTORS

Genetic evidence confirms that chickens were domesticated from jungle fowl, of which there are four species (gray, Ceylon, green, and red). There has been much dispute as to which species of jungle fowl contributed genetic material to the modern chicken.

In the red, gray, and Ceylon species, the comb is a single, upright, and serrated blade, and there is a pair of wattles, much like the "typical" domestic chicken. In contrast, the green jungle fowl has an unserrated blade, multicolor comb and only one wattle.

Charles Darwin was convinced from his studies that the red jungle fowl was the only ancestor of the domestic chicken. However, it has recently been demonstrated that the modern chicken's gene for yellow skin most probably came from the gray species.

KEY

- *Red jungle fowl*
- *Gray jungle fowl*
- *Ceylon jungle fowl*
- *Green jungle fowl*
- *Indus Valley*

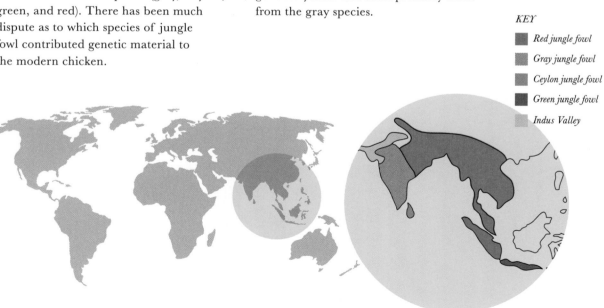

SPREAD OF THE DOMESTICATED CHICKEN

One genetic study suggests that all modern chickens may have descended from chickens domesticated in Thailand. However, it appears from more extensive studies that domestication occurred independently in different parts of Asia, and that chickens first domesticated in the Indus Valley then spread to Europe and Africa.

Analysis of DNA extracted from bones excavated on the coast of Chile suggests that there were chickens in the Americas before the arrival of Europeans. The bones in question were from chickens more closely related to Polynesian strains than chickens bred in Europe, and carbon dating indicates that they were discarded sometime between 1320 CE and 1410. If correct, this means that Polynesian explorers beat Columbus to the Americas by at least 100 years.

Above right *The red jungle fowl was thought to be the only ancestor of the chicken.*

Below *The gray jungle fowl may be the source of the gene for yellow skin.*

WHY JUNGLE FOWL?

Jungle fowl have several natural traits that predisposed them to becoming domesticated:

- They are seed and grass eaters, able to forage on their own, so do not have to compete with people for food.

- They cope well in many different climates and can survive a range of environmental conditions.

- They learn to recognize and follow a female parent bird in the wild—a process that is called "imprinting." Crucially, if the parent is not the first thing they encounter, they can also become imprinted on other animals or moving objects—including a human attempting to domesticate them (see pages 122–125).

The Chicken in History & Culture ~~

Archaeological and historical records indicate that when chickens were first domesticated it was for cultural rather than culinary purposes. As an increasingly common feature in everyday life, they were also quickly absorbed into the art and beliefs of the ancient world.

KEPT FOR SPORT

Cockfighting dates back to the earliest days of chicken domestication. It originated in the Far East and is known to have been popular in ancient Greece as long ago as 500 BCE. Like so much else in ancient Greek culture, the sport was adopted by the Romans, which, in turn, saw it spread throughout their empire.

The practice remained popular in Britain and North America right up until the nineteenth century, when it was outlawed, but it is still pursued in many other countries in the world. Cockfights are not always to the death, but often end with one of the cockerels being severely injured. In some forms, the cockerels' natural spurs are removed and replaced with metal spurs strapped to the legs.

Left *Greek relief panel from around the fifth century* BCE *featuring a cockerel.*

DEPICTED IN ART

The earliest images of chickens in Europe date back to pottery from the ancient Greek city-state of Corinth in the seventh century BCE. There are also references to chickens in ancient Greek poetry and plays, often describing them as "Persian birds," hinting at origins lying farther to the east. The bird is also a regular feature in Roman arts and crafts, such as terracotta lamps and mosaics.

INVESTED WITH MEANING

The humble chicken has been invested with great significance in various cultures, particularly thanks to the ubiquity of the cockerel's crow at first light. In Islam, for example, the messenger of Allah says, "When you hear the crowing of cocks, ask for Allah's blessings for they

have seen an angel." Likewise, in many central European folk tales, the first crow of a rooster marks the time for the devil to disappear, and in traditional Korean weddings, a male and female chicken are set on the wedding table wrapped in blue and red cloth to mark a new beginning.

In Christianity, the cockerel signifies a kind of vigilance, its crow announcing the denial of Jesus by his leading disciple. In the ninth century CE, to remind all Christians of that defining moment, every church in Europe was ordered to carry a symbol of a cock on its dome or steeple. This is what led to the commonly seen sight of the "weathercock."

In traditional Jewish practice, a chicken is often used for a ritual known as kapparos because it is a readily obtained source of kosher meat. In the ritual, which is performed on the afternoon before Yom Kippur (the Day of Atonement), the chicken is swung around a person's head and then slaughtered; the animal symbolically takes on the sins of the person performing the ritual and the meat is donated to the poor.

In Hindu cremation ceremonies, as they are performed in Indonesia, a chicken is also used to keep evil at bay. It is tethered by its leg throughout the ceremony to attract evil spirits away from the mourning party. However, instead of being killed at the end, the chicken is returned home to its normal life.

The Changing
Role of the Chicken

Domestication has undoubtedly affected the physique and behavior of chickens. They have, for instance, become bigger and heavier, and specialized breeding has led to a wider variety of plumage colors.

Their wings have also become even more superfluous. The ancestors of today's chickens did not fly great distances, only taking to the wing to escape potential predators and reach their roosting sites in trees. Today, some lighter chickens will fly short distances to explore, but most have practically abandoned flight. Domestic chickens are not obliged to spend as much time foraging as their wild ancestors, which may diminish their ability to fend for themselves.

Most historic breeds of chicken are "dual purpose," which means they are raised for both meat and egg production. It was only when commercial chicken farming intensified in the late 1950s that breeds were developed specifically for one purpose or the other (see pages 210–211).

Right *Chickens such as the Wyandotte are popular breeds.*

Below *The Leghorn breed is highly adapted to its common role as an egg producer.*

Some highly selected strains can reach slaughter weight in just five to six weeks, compared to twelve to sixteen weeks for other strains. Increased body weight puts further strain on the hearts and lungs of broilers, and their legs can get distorted.

Broilers have also been selected for an increased appetite. This becomes a problem for the birds saved from the slaughterhouse for the purposes of rearing young. Bred to have a large appetite, these birds must have their diets restricted in order to stop them from becoming overweight and unable to breed effectively. This means they constantly feel hungry, which can lead to behavioral and welfare problems.

AS AN EGG PRODUCER

Egg-laying breeds are selected for high egg productivity. They usually have small bodies, so that less energy is wasted on producing meat instead of eggs. The most popular breed that produces white-shelled eggs is the Leghorn, and the most popular brown-shell producer is the Rhode Island Red.

BACKYARD CHICKENS

Some dual-purpose breeds remain and are often favored by backyard chicken keepers. Smaller and more decorative birds are also kept for pleasure. Chickens make excellent pets. They can also serve to reduce the need for pesticides and herbicides on a homestead by eating insect pests and weeds and providing fertilizer for crops in the form of nitrogen-rich manure.

AS A MEAT PRODUCER

Broilers are chickens raised specifically for meat production; they are highly efficient at converting feed into meat. They were initially bred by mating a Cornish strain of cockerel that was naturally "double breasted" with a hen of a tall, large-bone variety of Plymouth Rock. They have since been further selected to grow rapidly to a large size.

The Chicken of Tomorrow

International competition and the high cost of modern breeding, marketing, and distribution programs have led to selective breeding, with commercial chickens now having less than half the genetic diversity of their wild counterparts. Researchers have found that commercial broilers come from just three lines of chicken, and egg layers are from only one specialized line.

Traits deemed undesirable today may largely be phased out; however, this is with unknown consequences for the future and may lead to commercial chickens being vulnerable to new diseases, so the ethical and welfare implications are of paramount importance. In such circumstances, hobby farmers may play an increasingly vital role in maintaining the diversity of the gene pool.

WHAT MIGHT FUTURE CHICKENS LOOK LIKE?

It has jokingly been suggested that a four-legged hen would serve a far more useful purpose than one with two legs and two wings; it could still lay eggs, but it would provide far more meat. Tempting although this may sound to breeding companies, there are practical as well as ethical problems to overcome. Four-legged chicks, for example, are occasionally hatched naturally (although the extra pair of legs is additional to, instead of replacing, the wings). Importantly, the extra legs do not get used, which means that the muscles, and the meat they represent, do not develop properly. Nevertheless, genetic engineering has also been applied to produce four-legged chickens with no wings, so the possibility of their development remains.

It has also been suggested that it would be more efficient to breed chickens without feathers—so-called "preplucked" chickens. Again, this is not as outlandish as it sounds. The genetic mutation resulting in a featherless chicken occurred naturally many decades ago. Today, there is interest in breeding broiler chickens with this feature; they would not only be preplucked but would also be less prone to heat stress.

Right *Featherless chickens have been known to occur naturally.*

GENETIC ENGINEERING

It is probable that the chicken of the near future, at least, will not look any different to the chicken that we are familiar with today. For now, industrial chicken breeders are content to focus on harnessing the power of genetic engineering to create ever more efficient birds. There are several avenues that are being pursued.

A good deal of work is being done to identify DNA markers for various desirable and undesirable chicken traits. If a breeding company can know more about a particular chicken's DNA, it can more accurately assess its suitability as a breeding specimen.

The relatively new field of transgenics is also being considered. A transgenic animal is one that has had a gene or genes transferred into its genome from another organism. One hope is that transgenic chickens could be developed to produce pharmaceutical medicines or other proteins in their eggs. Another is that a strain of chicken could be created with an immunity to deadly diseases such as avian influenza.

A third possibility is that the chickens of the future won't just look the same as they do today—they may all look the same as each other, too. At least two of the main chicken breeding companies are known to be pursuing the cloning of chickens on an industrial scale.

Below *Both these chickens are eight weeks old but their difference in size shows how much breeding can affect growth.*

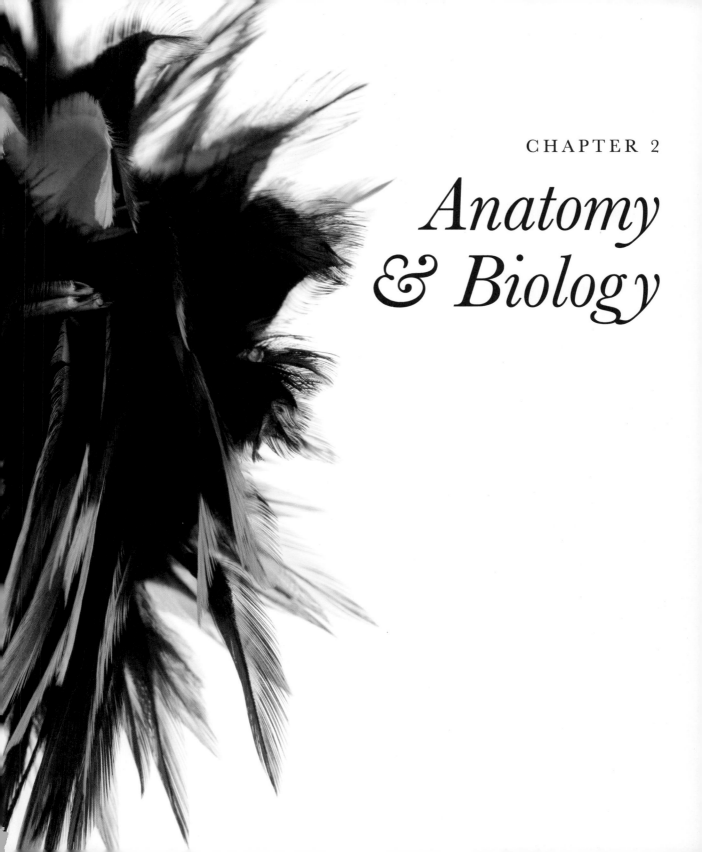

CHAPTER 2

Anatomy
& Biology

The Skeleton 〰

Although chickens have been domesticated for thousands of years, their anatomy remains largely that of their jungle-fowl ancestors. As with any bird, the chicken's skeleton has to be strong enough to support its weight and allow for it to walk, but also light enough to make flight possible. This remains true today, although many modern chicken breeds rarely take to the wing (see pages 50–51).

TYPES OF BONE

There are three main types of bone found in the chicken skeleton, each with its own tell-tale structure.

The bones that provide strength are referred to as cortical bones.

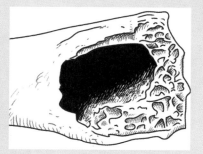

Pneumatic bones contain a light honeycomb structure of cavities filled with air. These cavities are connected to air sacs, which are connected to the lungs, meaning that pneumatic bones assist with both flight and breathing. Bones of this type include those in the skull, the keel, clavicle, humerus, and the lumbar and sacral vertebrae. They are much more easily broken than cortical bones.

About 10 to 14 days before a laying period, some bones undergo a change so that they can provide calcium for egg-shell formation. Such bones, which include the tibia and femur, are described as medullary; they have been found only in birds and dinosaurs.

CHICKEN SKELETON

WING/FORELIMB

The forelimb has evolved into a wing that no longer bears the chicken's weight; many of the names of the bones are, therefore, familiar (such as shoulder, carpus, metacarpus, and phalanges). The metacarpus consists of three bones, two of which are fused together. There are only three phalanges (instead of five), two of which fuse to form one digit (similar to a rudimentary finger). The third forms a thumblike structure. The scapula has also adapted for flight; it is fused with the coracoid bone and clavicles to form a structure known as the furcula (the wishbone).

SPECIALIZED BACKBONE

The chicken's backbone contains several special features:

- Fourteen neck/cervical vertebrae (double the number found in mammals) are movable, which allows for movements, such as pecking for food.

- Seven body/dorsal vertebrae are fused to support the wings, and the last two vertebrae are fused to the pelvis.

- Seven lumbar and seven sacral vertebrae are fused together and to the pelvic bones. The pelvic bones have no inferior fusion, thus creating a large opening for egg laying.

- Seven tail/coccygeal vertebrae are either movable, helping to provide directional flight, or, in the case of the last few vertebrae, fused together to allow for a solid base for the tail feathers.

LEG/HIND LIMB

The tarsometatarsal bones of the leg/hind limb are fused together. There are usually only four digits (five in some breeds); in the male, a spur is also present. The legs are placed farther forward toward the bird's center of gravity, which allows for greater stability, a much needed attribute when bipedal (that is, standing on only two legs).

CALCIUM DEFICIENCY

Chickens need a diet high in calcium to make up for the amount lost during egg production. If not, calcium will be drawn from cortical bone, which can cause osteoporosis and make fractures more probable. It may be necessary to treat serious cases of calcium deficiency (also referred to as "caged layer fatigue" or "rickets") with calcium phosphate, vitamin D3, or medicine prescribed by a veterinarian.

Muscles

Most muscles that are present in mammals are also present in the chicken, but their size, complexity, and type can differ in order to achieve flight and a bipedal stance.

MUSCLES FOR MOVEMENT

The contraction and relaxation of muscles is what allows the body to move. As with many other species, the chicken achieves this by using three key muscle types:

Cardiac muscle

This causes the chambers of the heart to contract and relax, thus forcing blood around the body and creating the heartbeat.

Skeletal muscles

Muscles attached to the bones of the skeleton are used to control voluntary movement. Skeletal muscle is also found in the eye to allow for movement within this complex organ.

Smooth muscle

This is necessary for involuntary movement (movement that the chicken does not have to think about, such as for breathing). This includes the blood vessels and parts of the respiratory, urinary, reproductive, and digestive systems.

CORRECT HANDLING

The keel is prone to damage during handling. To prevent this, it is important to support the sternum and legs with one arm underneath the chicken, and cover the wings with the other hand. Don't hold the chicken too tightly; its sternum must have room to move for the bird to breathe properly.

Right *Chickens reared for meat instead of eggs are bred—and fed—to have larger muscles. This can cause metabolic disorders and musculoskeletal dysfunction, such as myopathy (where muscle fibers do not function well, if at all). The resulting reduction in mobility can affect the welfare of these breeds.*

MUSCLE & MEAT

The muscles of a chicken can be classified as red or white, corresponding to dark and light meat, respectively. Red meat usually contains more fat and a protein called myoglobin-a, which carries iron and oxygen. The amount of myoglobin-a and fat within different muscles rises, depending on how much use they get. The leg muscles of domesticated chickens are usually more active than the chest muscles used in flying; the leg meat is, therefore, darker than the breast meat. The reverse is true for wild birds that fly more frequently. Broiler chickens also have muscles lighter in color than layer chickens.

CHICKEN MUSCLES

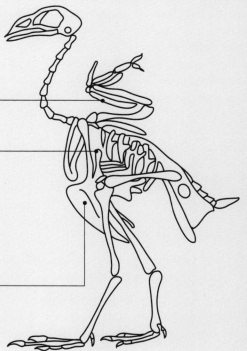

PECTORAL MUSCLES

The chest muscles, also called pectoral muscles, produce the downbeat of the wings (as indicated here) during flight. To achieve this, they are extremely large and powerful in relation to the chicken's overall size.

PERFORATED CONNECTIVE TISSUE

The muscular diaphragm found in mammals is absent in birds. The cavity is partitioned instead by perforated connective tissue, which allows for communication between the cavities and the air sacs. This, in turn, helps to keep down the body weight of the bird, helping to make flight possible. The respiratory muscles contract to move the sternum when both inhaling and exhaling air. This is in contrast to most other animals, where muscles contract to allow for air in but simply relax to exhale.

STERNUM BONE AND KEEL

The pectoral muscles attach to the sternum bone, which itself is also enlarged. The sternum also has a large midline keel to provide good sites for muscle attachment.

Heart & Circulation

The circulatory system of chickens shares some characteristics with that of mammals, but a different evolutionary path has led to some interesting points of variation.

THE ROLE OF BLOOD

Blood vessels are spread throughout the body and are essential in making sure that the entire body receives oxygen. Blood accounts for about 8 percent of the body weight in chicks and 7 percent in the adult chicken.

In addition to carrying oxygen, the blood must transport carbon dioxide, metabolic waste products, nutrients, hormones, water, and cells of the immune system around the body. It also plays a role in regulating the body temperature of the bird.

HEARTS COMPARED

Fish, amphibians, and reptiles have only two heart chambers, whereas birds and mammals have four. It is thought that birds and mammals evolved this attribute completely independently of one another.

The chicken heart has smoother walls and less complex valves than the human heart, allowing blood to flow more easily.

Compared to mammals of a similar size, birds have a larger heart, lower heart rate, and a greater cardiac output (the volume of blood being pumped by the heart each minute).

6) *Carbon dioxide is released from the lungs and oxygen diffuses into the blood. The circuit is completed when the blood is returned to the left atrium. The left ventricle is bigger because it has to pump the blood all the way around the body, whereas the right ventricle only has to get the blood to the nearby lungs.*

5) *The blood then flows into the right ventricle, which contracts to send the deoxygenated blood through the respiratory system.*

4) *After the blood has delivered oxygen to the tissues, it returns to the heart via a network of tiny venules, small veins, and finally large veins called the caudal vena cava and a pair of cranial venae cavae. These deliver the blood back from the body and head, respectively, into the right atrium of the heart.*

CIRCULATORY SYSTEM

Heart rate varies between different breeds, but it is generally around 200–350 beats per minute, with larger chickens usually at the lower end. Stress can have a large effect; dropping a day-old chick, for example, can cause the heart rate to increase from around 300 to 560 beats per minute. Even exposure to bright light can cause increased heart rate in chickens.

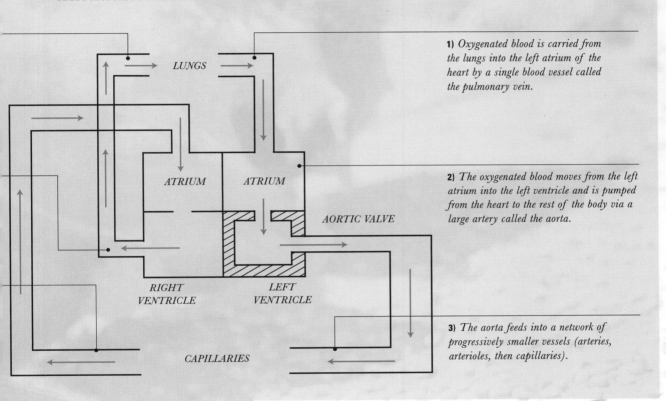

1) *Oxygenated blood is carried from the lungs into the left atrium of the heart by a single blood vessel called the pulmonary vein.*

2) *The oxygenated blood moves from the left atrium into the left ventricle and is pumped from the heart to the rest of the body via a large artery called the aorta.*

3) *The aorta feeds into a network of progressively smaller vessels (arteries, arterioles, then capillaries).*

LUNGS

ATRIUM   ATRIUM

AORTIC VALVE

RIGHT VENTRICLE   LEFT VENTRICLE

CAPILLARIES

BLOOD CELLS

As with humans, two main cell types are found within the blood—red and white. White blood cells are used to fight disease and illness, and red blood cells transport oxygen. Both cell types are produced in the spleen, which is in the abdomen near the gizzard. Red blood cells are also stored there until needed. The red blood cells of chickens differ from those of most mammals; they are ovoid instead of biconcave in shape, and they contain a nucleus (the control center of the cell). The red blood cells of other nonmammalian vertebrates (animals with a backbone) also contain a nucleus, but most are smaller than those of the chicken.

Respiratory System

The main role of the respiratory system is to introduce oxygen into the body and remove waste carbon dioxide. These are transported around the body via the heart and blood vessels. Chickens employ an efficient combination of two methods to obtain their oxygen, allowing for them to indulge in highly energetic activities, such as flying and running.

Air enters through the nostrils, and then passes through the pharynx and trachea. The trachea is relatively long and wide because the neck of a chicken has to be long and mobile in order to let the bird peck, preen, and build its nest.

Due to the length and width of the trachea, breathing rates of chickens are relatively low, because the total amount of air admitted in one breath is relatively high. A rooster takes around 18–20 breaths a minute, a hen 30–35.

Two flaps of tissue (the larynx) protect the opening of the trachea, making sure that food does not enter the airway when the chicken is swallowing.

In other species, the larynx also assists with noise production, but in birds a structure called the syrinx (voice box) is present at the end of the trachea. The passage at this point is surrounded by

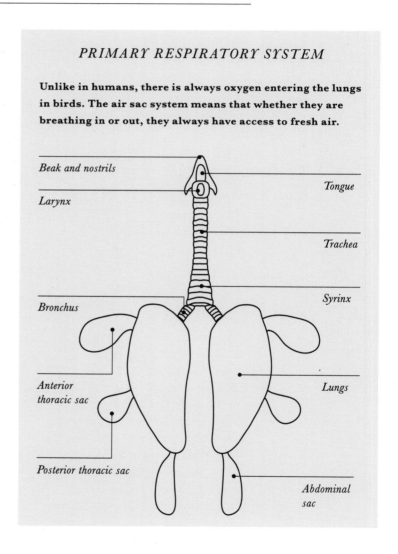

PRIMARY RESPIRATORY SYSTEM

Unlike in humans, there is always oxygen entering the lungs in birds. The air sac system means that whether they are breathing in or out, they always have access to fresh air.

Beak and nostrils

Larynx

Bronchus

Anterior thoracic sac

Posterior thoracic sac

Tongue

Trachea

Syrinx

Lungs

Abdominal sac

membranes, and when the membranes vibrate, a sound is produced.

The trachea branches into smaller tubes called bronchi, which enter the lungs. Secondary bronchi then branch off, each one in turn leading into hundreds of loops called parabronchi.

This system creates a large surface area within the relatively small space of the lung, making the absorption of oxygen as efficient as possible.

The lungs are attached to the ribs and only expand a little when air is breathed in—not like our own lungs, which expand like balloons when air enters. This is partly because the rib cage in the chicken has to be far more rigid than in mammals to provide a strong anchoring point for the large flight-enabling muscles.

When the chicken exhales, the air heads out through the trachea and through the nostrils. On its way, it passes over a series of complex bones and membranes, which serve to extract and absorb water from the air. This is essential to prevent dehydration occurring in hot environments.

RESPIRATORY HEALTH

Air quality is very important when considering chicken housing, because humidity, dust, bacteria, and ammonia in the air from manure will all affect chicken respiration and excessive levels can lead to illness.

SECONDARY RESPIRATORY SYSTEM

In addition to the relatively familiar trachea and lung system, the avian secondary bronchi also lead into separate air sacs, and from there into the pneumatic bones. These bones provide a secondary route by which air exchange can occur. The air sacs that connect the lungs to the pneumatic bones have very thin walls; they act like bellows to pull air into the relatively rigid lungs. There are several air sacs within the chicken's body.

Digestive System

The chicken digestive system is made up of the mouth, esophagus, stomach, intestine, cloaca, and anus. The liver and pancreas also play vital related roles.

THE MOUTH

The bird's mouth is made up of a beak and tongue, but no teeth. The upper part of the beak is fused with the bones of the head but is mobile, so it is more active in the eating process than the lower part. The tongue moves the food from the mouth into the esophagus, a canal with an extended area called the crop, found at the bottom of the neck. Seed-eating birds, such as domestic fowl, usually have a well-developed crop. A mucous fluid is released naturally into the crop and esophagus via glands to lubricate and soften food as it moves down the digestive tract.

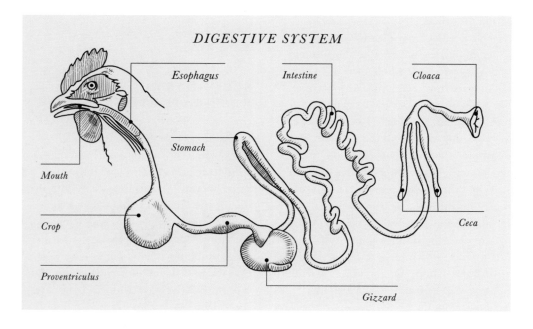

DIGESTIVE SYSTEM

Esophagus · Intestine · Cloaca · Mouth · Stomach · Crop · Ceca · Proventriculus · Gizzard

THE STOMACH

Once the food has moved out of the crop and all the way down the esophagus, it enters the stomach. The stomach has two compartments; the proventriculus and the gizzard. The wall of the proventriculus contains glands that secrete hydrochloric acid and enzymes to break down and digest the food. The gizzard is made up of strong muscular tissue, which grinds the food. To help this process, chickens swallow grit or stones, which collect within the gizzard and provide a hard surface against which tough food items, such as seed casings, can be broken down.

Together, the gizzard and grit perform the role that teeth play in other animals. Most commercial fowl foods contain grit, but chickens may still naturally swallow small stones or wood shavings.

THE INTESTINE

Once food exits the stomach, it is squeezed through the small intestine by a process of muscular contractions called peristalsis. To break the food down further, it is acted upon by bile from the liver and secretions from the pancreas.

Two "ceca" sacs, each about 6 inches (15 cm) long, are situated at the junction between the small and large intestine. These contain bacteria that assist in breaking down the food. The large intestine consists of a short rectum, which helps to reabsorb water from the various digestive secretions, and the cloaca, which links the chicken's digestive, urinary, and genital tracts. Chickens do not urinate in the typical sense. Instead, the waste is ejected with the feces as solid uric acid (the white substance seen in the feces).

READING THE CROP

The crop of a chicken sits just beneath its neck, in the center or slightly to the right-hand side of the chicken's breast. By observing and feeling for changes in the crop, you can make a number of simple health checks:

If the crop is swollen, the chicken has been eating; if not, it may be off its food.

If the chicken has had a large meal, the crop may naturally extend a little, but this will reduce over the following few hours.

If the crop remains swollen and feels solid to the touch, there may be compacted food stuck in there, which can be fatal. Give warm water, melted butter, vegetable or olive oil, or yogurt to move the blockage. Gently massage the crop to move the food. If this does not work, seek veterinary help.

If the crop feels full of water and the chicken's breath smells foul, it may have sour crop, a fungal infection that occurs if the crop is not fully empty overnight. Massage the crop while holding the bird upside down to remove the food. Feed the bird yogurt with live cultures to fight the infection; the chicken may need an antifungal prescription.

Male Reproductive System ～

The male chicken has a pair of testes situated close to the kidneys. Before sexual maturity, they weigh about ⅛ ounce (3 g) but during the breeding season they increase dramatically in size, reaching a maximum of about 1 ounce (30 g).

Hormones produced in the testes promote the development of behavior patterns, such as aggression and mating, and physical attributes, such as comb growth and sperm production. In contrast to mammals, sperm production in chickens can occur at normal body temperature, which means that the testes can remain in position close to the kidneys, instead of in a slightly cooler external scrotum.

Sperm are released from each testis along a deferent duct, together with a small amount of fluid. The two deferent ducts open into the cloaca. The phallus of a rooster contains erectile tissue, which forms a groove along which the sperm can travel from the cloaca to the surface of the phallus.

The phallus itself does not protrude from the rooster's body but is pressed against the female once the male has mounted her (see pages 86–87).

MALE CHICKEN REPRODUCTIVE ORGANS

Testes

Vas deferens

Kidney

Ureter

Cloaca

The diagram shows chromosome inheritance:

HEN (Z W) × ROOSTER (Z Z)

Offspring:
- Z Z → ROOSTER
- Z Z → ROOSTER
- Z W → HEN
- Z W → HEN

CHICKEN GENETICS

The chicken has thirty nine pairs of chromosomes inside the nuclei of its cells. The genes on these chromosomes control the correct development and function of these cells. They are important for determining visible features, such as feather and comb coloration, skin color, and body shape, as well as other desirable characteristics, such as egg laying, meat production, and egg size. In the world of commercial chicken breeding, genetic crossing is a vital way to obtain, retain, and refine these traits.

Of the pairs of chromosomes, one pair is called the "sex chromosomes" (Z and W); these determine gender. Each body cell in the male bird contains two copies of the Z chromosome, but the sperm carries just one copy. Normal cells in the female have both a Z and a W chromosome, but the female bird can only pass on either a Z or a W chromosome to her offspring. The resulting chick will, therefore, be ZZ (male) or ZW (female). It is, therefore, the female bird that is responsible for the sex of the chick. This is in contrast to many species, where the male usually carries differing sex chromosomes (in the human, these are the X and Y chromosomes, where XY = male and XX = female).

EFFECT OF DAYLIGHT

The reproductive capacity of the male chicken increases with exposure to daylight. The longer the day, the greater the rooster's capacity. Males should not be kept in stimulating light conditions unless they are about to be used for breeding.

Above *A rooster's reproductive organs do not protrude from the body.*

Female Reproductive System ～

Every female chicken has a single functioning ovary, which looks like a bunch of grapes. The ovary contains follicles of differing sizes and maturity. When each follicle matures, it is called a yolk or vitellus. The yolk then travels from the ovary into the oviduct. The oviduct contains five sections: infundibulum, magnum, isthmus, uterus, and the vagina.

The hen will lay a sterile egg if she has not mated with a rooster in the previous three to four weeks. If the egg is fertilized, a small dark spot will be present on its surface. A hen will generally lay eggs for a few days and then interrupt this cycle by at least one day of nonegg laying. In this manner, a domestic chicken may produce more than 300 eggs a year.

Hens that reach maturity in spring usually lay eggs earlier than those that reach maturity in the fall. Reducing the number of hours that light is provided will also decrease the number of eggs laid by chickens.

When keeping backyard chickens, it is a good idea to provide hens with nest boxes. This ensures that fewer eggs are broken and makes egg collection less labor intensive.

Below *It takes little more than 24 hours for a hen to create and lay an egg.*

THE PATH OF EGG CREATION

INFUNDIBULUM

If the hen has recently mated, sperm can survive in this section of the oviduct for about three to four weeks. The egg stays here for around 15 minutes and can be fertilized if sperm is present.

MAGNUM

The egg stays here for about three hours while the white is secreted.

ISTHMUS

The egg stays here for one hour while two membranes form around it.

UTERUS

The egg stays here for about 24 hours while the shell is formed.

VAGINA

The egg is carried from here to the cloaca and laid. A hormone called arginine vasotocin induces uterine contractions in order to deliver the egg.

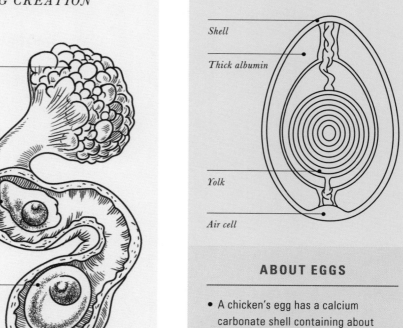

Shell

Thick albumin

Yolk

Air cell

ABOUT EGGS

- A chicken's egg has a calcium carbonate shell containing about 7,000 tiny pores to allow air into the embryo. The same pores can also let disease in, so care must be taken to prevent this.

- Hens require calcium to create their egg shells. If they cannot obtain enough calcium from their diets, they will start to use their own bones as a resource—causing a condition known as osteoporosis.

- If an egg is intended for human consumption, and you are unsure of its freshness, place ½ cup (130 g) of salt into 3¾ cups (870 ml) of water. If the egg sinks when you put it in this solution, it is fresh; if it sinks only partway, it is questionable; and if it floats, it is not fit to eat.

The Immune System ~~~

The purpose of the immune system is to fight off an infection. The chicken has two broad classes of defense—nonspecific and specific. The latter offers general protection, while the former deals with particular pathogens, such as bacteria, viruses, and parasites.

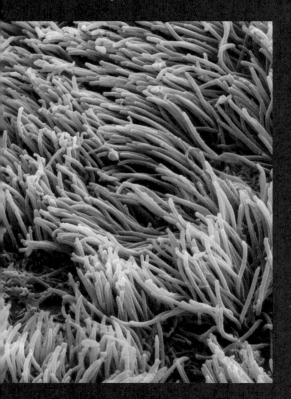

NONSPECIFIC IMMUNITY

The chicken benefits from a variety of nonspecific protective features:

Body temperature—chickens have a higher body temperature than mammals, making them too hot for some pathogens.

Skin—this acts as a barrier to infection (see pages 40–41). Any compromise to the skin (e.g. a wound) may allow pathogens to penetrate. A diet rich in biotin (also known as vitamin H) is essential for healthy skin formation—if not enough is available, skin sores develop. The best source of biotin for chickens is corn.

Respiratory epithelium—these are highly specialized skin cells lining the respiratory tract. Some secrete mucus to trap dust and disease-bearing organisms as they are inhaled. Others have fine, hairlike projections called cilia, which beat in unison to sweep mucus and particles up away from the lungs. If there are high levels of dust or ammonia in a henhouse, this so-called "mucociliary elevator" can be overwhelmed and become ineffective.

Left *Electron micrograph of ciliated epithelium in a lung.*

Microflora—many bacteria live on the skin and in the digestive system of healthy chickens without causing any harm, even aiding with digestion (they are called commensal bacteria). They also make it harder for disease-causing bacteria to gain a foothold. However, commensal bacteria can cause infection if the skin is damaged or the immune system fails to keep them in check, should it be weakened by fighting another illness.

SPECIFIC IMMUNITY

The specific—or adaptive—immune system involves various different cell types—some carried around the body in the blood or via lymphatic vessels, others residing in tissues:

Macrophages—these cells engulf material foreign to the body, including bacteria and protozoa, and release chemical messengers to alert other immune cells that the body is under attack. They also display parts of the pathogen that they have destroyed (antigens) on their surface to "present" to other immune cells.

Lymphocytes—these are white blood cells that specifically recognize presented antigens of invading organisms as being "nonself."

T-lymphocytes—one type orchestrates the cellular immune response by releasing messenger molecules; another produces powerful enzymes that kill infected body cells to prevent replication of the pathogen.

B-lymphocytes—these cells produce antibodies that bind onto pathogens in order to stop them from invading cells.

Memory cells—these remain in the body for a long time after an infection is cleared, ready to mount a rapid response if the same pathogen returns.

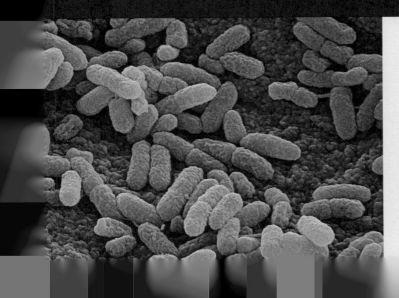

VACCINATION

Deliberately exposing chickens to a killed or disabled pathogen (or a part of it) primes the chicken to respond rapidly and fight off that pathogen before it can cause disease. Vaccines are available to protect chickens against potentially deadly diseases, such as Marek's disease, fowl pox, Newcastle disease, salmonella (pictured left), and coccidiosis. Some vaccines can be given in drinking water, others have to be injected.

The Skin ~

The chicken's skin is mostly thin and features only one secretory gland hidden away near the bottom of the tail. This is called the uropygial gland (commonly known as the oil or "preen" gland).

In preening, the chicken picks up oil by rubbing its head on the gland, which usually has a tuft of specialized feathers on it that acts as a brush; it then uses its head to transfer the oil onto the rest of its feathers. The oil serves to keep the feathers clean and dry and also has a waterproofing effect (see pages 66–69).

Other specialized structures associated with the skin include the comb and wattles, earlobes, scales on the legs and toes, spurs, claws, and the beak.

SKIN COLOR

Chickens with yellow skin have carotenoid pigments in their diet (such as from corn and alfalfa). Black skin is due to melanin (the same pigment that determines the color of human skin), which is made in specialized skin cells. White skin, which lacks any pigments, is a dominant trait over yellow skin, but broiler chickens have been selected to have yellow skin, because this is what consumers prefer. However,

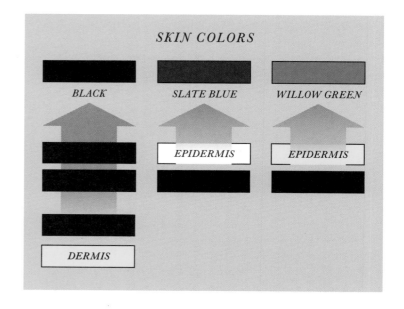

SKIN COLORS

BLACK   SLATE BLUE   WILLOW GREEN

EPIDERMIS   EPIDERMIS

DERMIS

even with the right genes, there has to be enough carotenoid pigment in the diet for the skin to turn yellow.

The color of the shanks is determined by pigments in the upper (epidermis) and lower (dermis) layers of the skin. Melanin in both layers gives the darkest shanks, and melanin in the epidermis obscures any yellow in the dermis. A white epidermis over a black dermis produces a slate blue color, and a yellow upper layer over a black lower layer results in willow green.

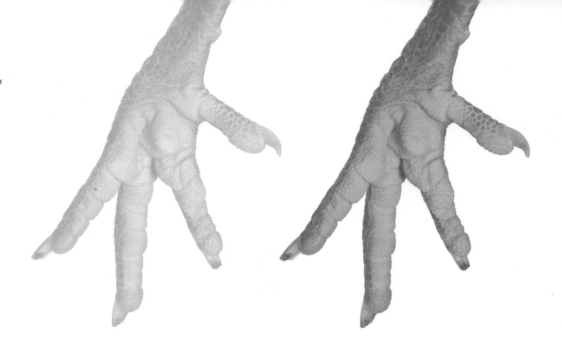

SKIN COLOR AS AN INDICATOR OF LAYING

Yellow-skinned breeds of chicken start to lose their pigment during the laying period because it is diverted to the egg yolk. The vent is the first area to be affected, so a white or pink vent indicates that a hen is laying. The loss of pigment then progresses sequentially to the eye ring, earlobes, beak (from the base to the tip), and finally to the lower part of the leg – the shanks (from front to back). Bleached shanks suggest that a chicken has been in continuous egg production for at least fifteen to twenty weeks.

The pigment reappears in the same order as it went, so a hen that stopped laying two or three weeks ago may have a beak with a yellow base and colorless tip.

MAINTAINING HEALTHY SKIN

Chickens can easily become affected by mites and lice. Effects vary, but they can include skin irritation, sores, and crustiness. Providing a dust bath with added diatomaceous earth (a fine, mildly abrasive powder made from rock) helps chickens to get rid of such external parasites. If the problem persists, or you notice mites and lice on a chicken's feathers or skin, consult your veterinarian.

Left *Chicken infested with mites—note the loss of feathers and irritated skin around the comb.*

Feathers

Feathers define a bird as a bird. They are essential for flight; although not all birds fly, they provide protection and warmth, and they determine the bird's outward appearance.

A chicken looks very different without its feathers. When it is plucked, you can see that the feathers are not evenly distributed; they are arranged in distinct areas called feather tracts (pterylae). There are four main types:

Contour feathers

These are the largest feathers, which give the chicken its shape and color and provide protection against the elements. In contour feathers, the upper barbules have a series of hooks and the lower ones are slightly convex so that adjacent barbs are lightly "zipped" together. When a chicken is preening, running the beak along the feather zips up any sections of the feather that have come apart.

Contour feathers include the large flight feathers of the wing (remiges) and the tail feathers (retrices). Tail feathers have vanes of equal size. On flight feathers, the outer vane, which is on the leading edge of the wing and subjected to greater stresses in flight, is narrower.

Above *A semiplume*

Right *A slightly damaged contour feather shed from the wing (one vane is narrower than the other).*

Below *A downy feather*

Downy feathers

These feathers have a short shaft and soft barbs that do not interlock, making them "fluffy." They are important in protecting the chicken against the cold.

Semiplume

This is an intermediate type of feather between downy and contour feathers.

Filoplume

These feathers have a long, slender, soft rachis with only a few barbs at the very tip. They are scattered among the contour feathers and have sensory receptors at their base. It is, therefore, thought that the receptors on these feathers provide feedback on what is happening with the contour feathers.

APPEARANCE

There is huge variation in the appearance of modern chicken breeds. In addition to different plumage colors and patterns, some genetic mutations have been selected for their unusual look, giving rise to "silkie" chickens, whose feathers lack barbicels (the hooked projections that interlock the barbules) thus making them look fluffy, "frizzled" fowl, and chickens with feathers on their shanks and feet.

MOLTING

Feathers are usually renewed annually as they become battered and worn out. The timing and rate of molting is influenced by numerous factors, including the health of the bird, its diet, and its management.

In nature, chickens stop laying in late summer in plenty of time to molt and grow a new feather coat for winter. However, domestication has lengthened the laying period so that it often overlaps with molting. This has led to the mistaken conclusion that egg laying stops as a consequence of molting, causing farmers in some parts of the world to control molting to extend the laying life of the hen. As this entails withholding food and water, there are obvious welfare implications of doing this.

Feathers are lost in a particular order (from the head first, to the neck, body, and, finally, the wings and tail). The large wing and tail feathers are also replaced in order; thus they provide an estimate of how long a bird has been out of production. In high-producing hens, molting takes no longer than three months.

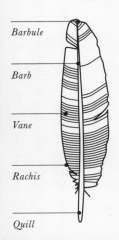

ANATOMY OF A FEATHER

Barbule

Barb

Vane

Rachis

Quill

The basic features of a feather are a hollow shaft (rachis) with side branches that form the vane; the part of the rachis where there are no side branches is called the calamus, or quill. Barbs branch from the main shaft and have additional branches called barbules. Most of the variation in the form and structure of feathers is due to differences in how the barbules and their branches are structured.

Wattles & Combs

Wattles vary in size, shape, and color, depending on the breed of chicken; combs even more so. Both begin to grow in the first few weeks after hatching. Because roosters usually have larger and more brightly colored combs than hens, observing their growth can indicate what sex a chick is.

Comb color also develops with age; when a young hen develops a bright red or pink comb, she is probably ready to begin laying eggs. A large, brightly colored comb is a sign of good health.

The "typical" single comb forms a straight line front to back on top of the head, with five to six points leading up to a thicker "blade."

Wattles usually consist of a single section hanging from each side of the beak. Rose wattles split into two sections.

Single

Pea

Strawberry

Crown

TEMPERATURE REGULATION

Because chickens do not sweat, wattles and combs are important for keeping them cool in hot weather (see pages 48–49). Their deep red color comes from a dense network of capillaries. These circulate blood from the comb to the wattles, which act like radiators, letting heat escape from the blood into the surrounding air.

A pea comb and small wattles are an advantage if chickens must endure a harsh winter climate. Hens usually sleep with their head tucked under a wing, but cockerels with large combs can be at risk of frostbite. Purple coloration can indicate poor circulation due to cold. Massaging affected areas with petroleum jelly can help blood flow return to the area and prevent frostbite. If frostbite does occur, tissue in the affected area may die, eventually turning black and falling off. Applying antibiotic ointment can reduce the risk of infection.

A chicken's wattle or comb can easily be damaged, either accidentally or in a fight. Because they cannot be repaired, the area should be cleaned thoroughly and antibiotic cream applied to minimize the risk of infection. The advice of a veterinarian should be sought on removing the damaged parts. The chicken should be isolated until the wound has healed.

COURTSHIP

The secondary function of the comb is to help a chicken attract a mate. There is a correlation between the size and color of the comb and levels of the "male hormone" testosterone in chickens. The "alpha" rooster (often the bird with the biggest, brightest comb) is able to mate with all the hens in a flock, thus making sure that the strongest, healthiest male passes on his genes to the next generation. In the absence of a rooster, the most dominant hen may grow a larger, brighter comb and even begin to crow.

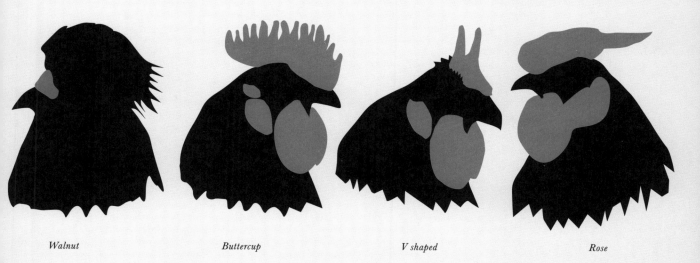

Walnut

Buttercup

V shaped

Rose

Sensory System ~

The chicken brain is six to eleven times larger than the brain of a reptile of a similar size. The difference in size is particularly marked in the cerebellum and optic lobes, which assist with vision and flight. Eyesight is extremely important to the bird; in fact, the eyes together weigh the same amount as the entire brain.

HOUSING

The housing environment is very important in maintaining chicken health and behavior, but also when considering the senses used. Pecking for food enables the bird to use sight, smell and touch, and adequate lighting allows the chicken to see better. Chickens also detect vibrations very well due to receptors in their skin and legs. When vibrations (such as movement from humans) are present, the chickens will become alert and send warning calls. Ensuring that the poultry live in an environment without continuous movement/vibrations will help the birds to stay calm.

VISION

A chicken's eyes are positioned on the side of its head, which extends its field of vision to over 300 degrees. This allows the bird to be an efficient lookout for potential predators. The eyes are protected by upper and lower eyelids, but also have a membrane that can move across the eye and protect the cornea.

Like humans, birds have three different types of cone on their retinas that allow them to see in color. Unlike humans, they also have a fourth cone that allows them to see in the ultraviolet (UV) range. Chickens have UV markings on their bodies that act as a cue for mating behavior. Therefore, if they are housed with fluorescent UV lighting, mating behavior and productivity will increase.

In addition to these attributes, chickens also have "rod cells" to help them see better in the dark, and recently discovered "double cones," which are thought to help them detect motion. Their all-round visual acuity lets them identify food, water, nesting sites, and locations to scratch. It also makes it possible for individuals to recognize each other, and, therefore, maintains social order within the group.

HEARING

Domestic fowl have around twenty different vocalizations with a wavelength ranging between 400 and 6,000Hz, so a good sense of hearing is important. Chickens duly have a hearing range of between 15-10,000Hz. It is also thought that the hen and brood communicate via body positioning and sound signals. The feathers surrounding the opening to the ear ensure that sound can travel into the ear.

SMELL

It is known that domestic fowl have olfactory receptors in their upper jaw and can, therefore, respond to particular scents. It is thought that this may assist when making food choices.

TOUCH

The sense of touch relies on "mechanoreceptors" in a part of the brain called the thalamus. These are the ends of sensory nerves that specialize in responding to pressure. They are important for monitoring touch via the beak, which has to make very fine movements when the bird is feeding, and via the feet when the bird is moving or scratching the ground.

Because the sensitivity of the beak is so important for feeding, nest building, grooming, and social interaction, care must be taken when tipping or trimming it as this can affect chickens' abilities to use their touch-based sensory systems.

Temperature is also monitored via cold and warm receptors in the skin, and pain/ unpleasant stimulation is detected via specialized nerve endings called nociceptors.

Thermoregulation

Temperature control is a vital factor when keeping chickens. It affects not only their welfare, behavior, and food consumption, but also their egg and meat production. Egg laying, for example, is reduced if the temperature reaches 80.6°F (27°C); a range of 70–75°F (21–24°C) is preferable.

COOLING MECHANISMS

Chickens do not have sweat glands, so other cooling mechanisms are important. The comb and wattles, nasal cavity, and mucosa in the trachea, lungs, and air sacs allow heat transfer and, therefore, cooling of the animal. Chickens also pant when they get hot and may shed their feathers. A hen will try to increase her surface area by drooping her wings away from the body, press plumage close to the body, eat less, produce fewer eggs, and grow less if the ambient temperature is too high.

HEATING MECHANISMS

If they are too cold, chickens may fluff out their plumage to trap a layer of air. Chickens more than three weeks old can also tremble when too cold; the activity of the muscular contractions generates heat.

HOUSING & MANAGEMENT

Birds with little space will more probably experience overheating, because they cannot move their wings to disperse heat. Heat stress can kill birds very quickly; in commercial units, birds can die within 15 minutes if cooling fans fail and the temperature rapidly increases. If the environmental temperature rises to 109°F (43°C), 30 percent of chickens will die.

Below *In cold weather, chickens will fluff out their feathers to trap warm air as close to their body as they can.*

When overheating is suspected, provide as much ventilation as possible, reduce the number of birds in small areas, and remove chicken feed to lower the metabolism of the birds and reduce the speed at which they overheat.

Birds kept in free-roaming or organic systems may not have artificial cooling systems in their houses. It is still important to make sure that the houses are well ventilated, and that high temperature alarms are fitted. If possible, birds should be able to escape a hot house by heading to a safe outdoor area, where there is a shaded location to protect them from direct sunlight.

TRANSPORTATION

Chickens can be exposed to hypothermia (getting too cold) or hyperthermia (getting too hot) when being transported. Depending on the weather conditions expected, providing good heating or ventilation is vital. Night-time transport should be considered in hot climates, and the number of chickens per crate should be kept to a minimum.

TEMPERATURE, INCUBATION, & HATCHING

Immediately following egg delivery, development of the embryo may be temporarily halted for up to ten days if the egg is kept at a temperature of 60–65°F (15.6–18.3°C). To encourage the embryo to resume growth and development, the egg should be gradually warmed to 75°F (23.9°C) over six to eight hours. Optimum development will then be achieved by incubating the eggs at 82.7–100°F (37.5–37.7°C) for the first nineteen days, followed by 97–99°F (36.1–37.2°C) for the final two days of incubation. Exact temperatures vary, depending on breed, egg size, shell quality, the age of the egg when it was incubated, and the humidity of the air.

Newly hatched chickens in artificial brooding conditions need 86–90°F (30–32°C) because they cannot control their body temperature effectively. This becomes dangerous if the environmental temperature is below 79°F (26°C).

IDEAL TEMPERATURE

The core body temperature of an adult chicken is about 107.4°F (41.9°C). The average adult white Leghorn chicken can maintain its body temperature when the environment is 30–98.6°F (-1–37°C), but opinion differs on what the ideal housing/outside temperature should be. Some say it should be 68–95°F (20–35°C), but others believe it should be 50–86°F (10–30°C).

Adaptations for Flight ~

Chickens are not prolific flyers. Larger breeds take to the wing rarely, if at all, but lighter ones will fly short distances, to reach a perch perhaps, or to forage for food beyond a small barrier. From an anatomical point of view, chickens have a variety of adaptations for flight—aside from their wings and feathers.

Flight (or extreme flapping) seems to be important in response to unexpected stimuli in the environment. Getting up high to roost is also something that chickens are motivated to do, which is aided by flight/flapping.

Some vertebrae have fused to allow extra strength to develop near the wings.

Other vertebrae near the tail have not fused, allowing it to act as a rudder during flight.

RESIDUAL BENEFITS

Whether or not chickens are actually required to fly, behavioral activities, such as preening and wing flapping, must be maintained in order to achieve maximum health. Research has shown that chickens in a perchery take, on average, twice as many steps as those housed in a cage and are also more likely to attempt flight. It has also been shown that placing birds in small cages without perches reduces bone strength by up to 85 percent. Caged birds are, therefore, twice as likely to break bones in comparison to free-roaming or perchery chickens.

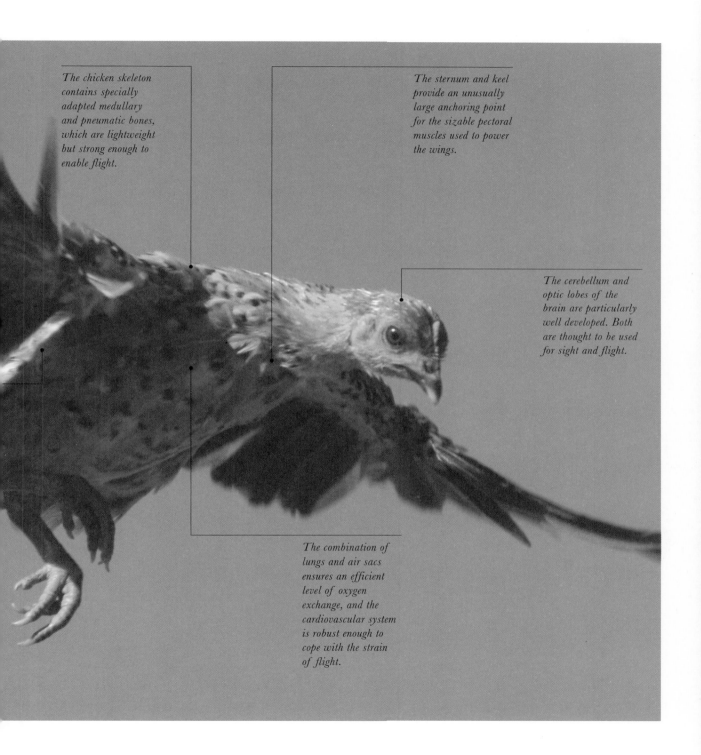

The chicken skeleton contains specially adapted medullary and pneumatic bones, which are lightweight but strong enough to enable flight.

The sternum and keel provide an unusually large anchoring point for the sizable pectoral muscles used to power the wings.

The cerebellum and optic lobes of the brain are particularly well developed. Both are thought to be used for sight and flight.

The combination of lungs and air sacs ensures an efficient level of oxygen exchange, and the cardiovascular system is robust enough to cope with the strain of flight.

CHAPTER 3

Behavior

Behavior of the Domestic Chicken

Today, most of the more than 20 billion chickens sharing the planet with us are kept for the meat or the eggs they produce. Still, it has been said that the ancestors of modern chickens first captured people's attention and interest because of their spectacular behaviors. Roosters will readily engage in ritual displays of their brilliant tail feathers and bright combs and wattles when competing with each other, and they will also rush into close-contact physical fights. In fact, it is likely that the domestication of fowl may have begun in order to breed superior contestants for cockfighting.

Thankfully, the days of blood sports are largely now in the past, and breeders have switched their attentions to other aspects of a chicken's appearance and behavior, such as their complex visual and vocal displays.

BEHAVIORS & DOMESTICATION

Many of the behaviors of the modern domesticated chicken were already present in their primary ancestor species, the red jungle fowl of South Asia:
- Both are polygynous, meaning that one male is sought out by multiple females for mating.
- Both are monoparental, meaning that only one of the parents (the mother) looks after the next generation.
- Each displays a strong social structure and order, imposed by the bonds established among females and the frequent competitive interactions between males.
- Jungle fowl have high predation rates upon their ground nests, and must replace lost clutches of eggs rapidly. Both wild and captive fowls are, therefore, highly fertile and have a copious laying rate.
- Both are poor flyers, but wild and domesticated fowl continue to seek high perches, tree branches, and other safe spots to spend the night-time.

Above *Roosters naturally behave in an attention-grabbing way.*

All these traits have made the domestication and breeding of chickens easier around rural human dwellings over thousands of years. In turn, several of these ancestral behavioral traits must be considered when dealing with mass breeding of modern chickens. Particular attention must be paid to population density, daily mobility, and access to roosting sites when designing humane housing for chickens.

BEHAVIORS & SCIENTIFIC PROGRESS

Birds have contributed to major leaps in scientific knowledge. Most birds, including chickens, are diurnal (active during the day), use colors and sounds to get around the environment and to communicate with each other, and form long-lasting bonds between parents and offspring, including teaching the next generation how to feed and to protect themselves.

Take, for example, the enduring question of the impact of nature (biology, genetic control) and nurture (experience, social learning) on the behavior of an individual. Scientists have made several advances in this field thanks to studies of development inside and outside the chicken egg.

The avian egg is easily examined without requiring invasive surgery to access the growing embryo. As a result of these studies, we now know that unhatched embryos can see and hear, and use these experiences to recognize and communicate with others outside the egg. In other words, behaviors that were once thought to be innate have now been shown to be learned. We also know more about what mother birds, and other animals, contribute to their young—both in terms of their genetic code and in the way they nourish and supply nutrients, vitamins, hormones, and antibacterial substances to their eggs to ensure successful growth in the egg and survival once outside the egg.

The many and various behaviors of chickens are both instructive and fascinating—from their earliest days inside the egg to their complex social interactions later in life.

Evolution & Domestication ⟲

What can the ancestors of modern chickens tell us about their behavior? Scientific studies of jungle-fowl behaviors in the wild are rare, because these birds spend most of their lives in the dense forest understory in India, the Malaysian peninsula, and on nearby island archipelagos.

Occasional sightings of wild jungle fowl near roads, in forest clearings, and at the feet of grazing livestock do occur, especially in the quieter morning hours. At other times, the shorter and sharper crow of the male, compared to the long-lasting crows of domesticated roosters, reveals the presence of a small fowl flock.

What we do know is that these wild fowl live in small harems of a handful of hens and a dominant rooster, with a few satellite subordinate males shadowing the main harem.

Such a social structure is not alien to behavioral ecologists, especially to primatologists, because some of our closest great ape relatives, including gorillas, live in similar, highly structured single male/multifemale societies. Perhaps that is why it is no surprise that many behavioral terms, including "alpha chicken" and "pecking order" have made their way from behavioral studies of the chicken into our popular language.

Below *The colors and behaviors of fowl ancestors closely resemble those of modern chickens.*

TAKING FLIGHT

Many fowl species of the avian galliform (chicken-like) order remain safe in their natural environment thanks to their relatively cryptic plumage colors. It may be somewhat surprising to the human observer, but even the brightly iridescent tail and wing feathers of male fowls and pheasants in the wild, when viewed against the bright green vegetation and smooth stems of the subtropical forest floor, become an effective camouflage.

When being hidden is not enough, jungle fowl rely first on their strong feet to propel themselves rapidly through the tropical thickets.

Finally, when facing fatal danger or settling in at dusk for the perils of night, most fowls readily use their wings to lift themselves up to a high perch away from terrestrial predators.

This need to roost in trees at a safe height is so common across galliform species that it has come to influence the pattern in which flight feathers are first grown and then molted across the life of all henlike species. Indeed, there is a strong pressure for even young and flightless chicks to become volant (flighted) soon after hatching and leaving the nest.

Accordingly, the flight feathers of many galliform chicks can be already fully developed at hatching (such as those of the Australian brush turkeys) or grow so fast as to become functionally ready to lift the chick off the ground within days. Peafowl young, for example, can reach the safety of high-up roosting branches for the night after as little as 72 hours.

SELFISHNESS IS NATURAL

One of the most puzzling aspects of
biological diversity is that the information
that encodes for the vast variation in
colors, sounds, smells, and displays in
nature is passed on from generation to
generation as a tiny double string of
genetic material. Recent advances in
DNA sequencing technology have allowed
the full-scale identification of the entire
genetic code of many lineages of viruses,
bacteria, plants, fungi, and animals.

Among birds, the first full genome
described in late 2004 was that of a
domestic hen. And yet, identifying
DNA sequences alone does not allow
us to fully understand how genes
influence appearance and behavior
and, vice versa, how appearances and
behaviors enhance the passing on of
genes to the next generation.

What we do know is that both genes
and individuals are selfish—they act
so as to increase their own chances to
survive and to reproduce. However, what
about a rooster who doesn't eat a newly
discovered pile of grubs himself but calls
to the hens in the yard to approach? Or a
mother hen who spots and calls out loud

Above *Male turkeys
are genetically selfish:
brothers form tight
groups to attract females
over rival groups of
unrelated males.*

Right *Male roosters
often share discovered
food with their hens who
are the future mothers of
their shared progeny.*

at the site of a hawk in the sky, thereby making herself more noticeable to the predator? How can these behaviors be considered selfish?

The answer lies in the group-living habits of both fowl ancestors and modern chickens. The harem-holding male benefits from sharing his food and, eventually, mating with well-nourished hens capable of laying larger eggs; the mother hen benefits from alerting her own young to rush to safety and from the reciprocal calls by other hens in the group when they themselves next spot a predator.

The principle of selfishness persists even in the face of such seemingly selfless acts because they ultimately increase the chance that such apparently altruistic individuals survive and breed successfully.

CARING FOR THE NEXT GENERATION

All birds require some type of parental care. This is because the avian embryo, inside the hard-shelled egg, only starts to develop when exposed to heat. Close relatives of fowls, the megapodes in Australia and on nearby island archipelagos, use the heat of rotting piles of vegetation or geothermal sands on the sides of volcanoes to warm and incubate their eggs.

Other birds, such as parasitic cuckoos which lay their eggs in other birds' nests, preincubate their eggs inside the oviduct, so that the embryo has already begun development at the time of laying and can hatch in advance of its nest mates. For cuckoos, this is beneficial, because they can then toss out all eggs or nest mates soon after hatching in order to monopolize the foster parents' provisions. Indeed, many wild relatives of chickens are themselves parasitic, including wild turkeys, sneaking an egg or two into the nest of others.

Domestic hens, too, are well known for using the nests of others, resulting in just a few sites where eggs are laid (making them easy to locate in the chicken coop). However, unlike the killer cuckoo chicks, fowl hatchlings do not benefit from hatching earlier or, especially, later than the rest of the clutch. This is because they are precocial (ready to leave the nest) and the mother tends to lead the chicks away from the nest only when most have hatched and their feathers have dried, leaving latecomers and unhatched eggs exposed to cold and predators.

Behavioral Differences between the Sexes ～

Female and male chickens not only appear different in size (females are typically smaller) and plumage (males are brighter), but have fundamentally different behavioral repertoires to assure their success throughout life.

Although males are essential for sexual reproduction, on a per-headcount basis, females have a more predictable value both biologically and commercially. Females lay eggs, often hundreds throughout their lives, and they also contribute to meat production in commercial operations. In contrast, most males, both in backyards and in industrial-scale farms, are simply unneeded and typically are cast away

(i.e. killed) by their keepers as early as their sex can be identified. Other males, even if they make it to adulthood, have to compete with each other. Most of them, therefore, lose out when vying for the role of the resident rooster to court and mate with local hens.

Hens, on the other hand, can always become egg producers and, in smaller-scale farms and home operations, turn into brooding mothers to incubate eggs and raise the young.

Right *Sexual dimorphism is the scientific term for the differences in the size and shape of females versus males.*

Above *Single parenting (monoparental care) is the norm in chickens, and many other fowls and pheasants, but it isn't in quail and partridge species.*

CHOOSY FEMALES & WILLING MALES?

Studying the mating patterns of fruit flies in the late 1940s, British scientist A. J. Bateman demonstrated that the reproductive success of females depends on mating with a fertile male, whereas the reproductive success of males depends on mating with as many females as possible. This general rule, called the Bateman paradigm, is thought to account for the behavioral evolution of willing males, ready to mate with available females, and choosy females, seeking to mate only with a high-quality male.

At first glance, this paradigm seems to apply clearly to domestic chickens, because the resident rooster readily mates with the flock-member females. In turn, mating with a high-quality, dominant, and hopefully fertile, male is critical for female chickens, because they receive no tangible paternal support for the young; hens scrape the nest site, incubate the eggs, and brood, protect, and lead the young to food. Thus, obtaining fertile sperm from a sexually attractive rooster will provide two types of benefits to the hen: her eggs will be viable and her own sons will be sexually attractive, too.

However, recent research on the mechanics of mating in domestic fowl has revealed that males, too, can be choosy; when mated with the same female repeatedly, these males gradually reduce the amount of sperm that they invest. This is no surprise because, under natural conditions, a male would typically have already fought its way to the leadership position of the harem of hens, thus already limiting the array of males with whom the females would mate otherwise.

In the same way, it has been shown that females in better condition, indicated by brighter and fleshier female combs, will probably receive more sperm per mating from the same males. Investing in these females—and in those that are new to the flock—will be beneficial for the male, because these females will use his sperm to lay more and larger eggs, which hatch at higher rates and yield healthier chicks, all sired by that resident rooster.

Feeding & Drinking

Feeding is at the core of chickens' daily activities, both in duration and frequency. Birds typically have body temperatures a few degrees higher than mammals of a similar size, supported by faster metabolic rates. Birds, therefore, need more fuel to maintain this status quo, which can be achieved by eating more, and more often.

Ancestral jungle fowls and modern chickens are both omnivores, with a shift from a predominantly insect-based diet in the wild (including a curious taste among jungle fowl for termites) to a more plant- and grain-based diet fed to captive chickens. Noncaptive chickens—in the backyard and among feral populations—revert to their ancestral preferences and show excitement at the sight and taste of beetles, grubs, and earthworms.

Chickens also consume soil, grit, and pebbles. This provides them with micronutrients and helps them break down larger food items in their muscular gizzard. Like all birds, chickens do not have teeth to masticate ingested items, nor do they tend to use their toes or claws to hold down and tear apart larger pieces of food. They do, however, handle and crush some food items with their beak to generate bites small enough to swallow.

Chickens also eat raw or cooked flesh and even eggs, including those of their own species, but there are side effects, such as increased aggression and egg eating in the communal laying hens. Chicks have a tendency to approach moving, live prey items, such as mealworms, soon after hatching, especially in response to maternal calls to attract them. Females also call to their chicks to point to immobile prey and other palatable items, including grains and plant materials, and the young quickly learn to peck on these as a tasty reward for having approached the calling mother hen.

Above *In the outdoors, chickens readily search for grubs and other live foods.*

REPLENISHING WATER

Despite their higher metabolic rate and body temperatures, birds are better at conserving water than mammals of a similar size. This is because nitrogenous waste is excreted by birds as nonaqueous uric acid (see page 33). In fact, many bird species do not often consume water at all, instead hydrating themselves from liquid-rich fruit and plant parts, or fleshy prey items. Many desert birds, including the Australian zebra finch, a common pet bird, metabolically recycle water when digesting seeds and other starchy foods and may go for weeks without taking a sip of water.

Chickens originate from wetter forests and, perhaps because they are typically kept on a dry main diet, do require access to water. In fact, fresh water should be provided at different locations to help reduce competitive interactions near the source. Chickens, like most birds, cannot siphon water directly into their esophagus, and drink instead by lifting their beaks to let gravity pull the water down.

Free access to water and electrolytes, but also to liquid-rich foods, including fruits and greens, is especially important

in the hot summer months if chickens are kept outdoors, or during other high heat conditions (see pages 48–49).

Having water readily available combats elevated environmental temperatures, replenishes water lost through panting, and counteracts water and electrolyte deficiency caused by higher rates of urine and feces production.

Right *Chickens rapidly learn to feed and drink from artificial sources in captivity, often by watching each other.*

Resting & Roosting

Chickens and related galliform species commonly fall prey to both terrestrial and aerial predators. Locating and securing a safe site for resting and sleeping are, therefore, of paramount significance for both wild and feral fowls, and it is seen as a consistent behavioral pattern in backyard and cage-kept birds, too.

Although most chickens tend to escape danger on foot, nocturnal resting and sleeping requires greater and more predictable security. In fact, roosting on a high perch is such a critical component of night-time behavior that humane designs for chicken cages now require a higher perch to be installed for roosting near the roof for the night. In chicken coops, ladderlike perches should allow even nonflying chickens to hop to preferred higher perches. In trees, chickens prefer to land on a high branch under some dense foliage, covered from above against both falling rain and being sighted by aerial predators.

For the first few nights after hatching, chicks are often led to the safety of the nest by their mother, but once their flight feathers have grown and broken through, the young too will join the rest of the flock in trying to perch up high.

SLEEPING TO PREPARE FOR THE NEXT DAY

The circadian rhythm, or the day–night cycle of the physiological and behavioral patterns of many organisms, including chickens, is based on an internal clock of molecular machinery, adjusted by external inputs of light and dark periods.

In chickens, the photoreceptors responsible for color and light vision in the eye are also involved in directing and adjusting the mechanisms guiding diurnal and nocturnal behaviors. In turn, sleep and rest are essential for the birds

Left *Resting and sleeping are essential components of daily life at any age during the lifespan of chickens.*

to get ready for the next day's activities: foraging, keeping vigilant, maintaining or improving social ranks, finding mates, and caring for the next generation.

Research on sleeping birds has also shown that, much like in humans, sleep is critical for consolidating and storing the previous day's memories. For songbirds, sleep is essential for memorizing and being able to copy the melody of their father's song. For young chicks, sleep helps to consolidate their memory of the object on which they have imprinted—usually

Finally, and again similarly to humans, melatonin is a powerful regulator of both going to sleep in chickens and the type and duration of different sleep cycles. On the one hand, melatonin injections make getting to sleep quicker in general. On the other, melatonin-induced sleep is qualitatively and quantitatively different from natural sleep in chickens. There are longer periods of slow-wave sleep while paradoxical sleep starts later and doesn't last as long (this is the equivalent of rapid eye movement [REM] sleep).

Above *Domestic chickens seek out and visibly enjoy being able*

Maintaining Appearances ~⌐

People tend to be attracted to pets whose communication behaviors resemble those of ours: bright coloration, melodious sounds, comforting touch. Birds use vision and sound as their primary modes of communication, but, of course, these traits have evolved mostly to attract mates and to intimidate competition.

In bird species, including chickens, visual displays by males of bright plumes and impeccable fleshy ornaments serve the same functions: to attract hens and to maintain dominance over other roosters.

All types of feather color, whether the deep greens of the tail or the brilliant whites of several strains, as well as the cryptic rusty hues of other strains, are caused by two major types of pigments—carotenoids and melanins—deposited and tightly structured into the nanostructure of the feather barbules.

However, these pigments do not alone explain the overall appearance of most plumages. There is also the quality of iridescence, caused when lightwaves reflected from the barbules interact with other lightwaves to generate new colors visible only from certain angles.

Feather structures, and hence colors, are dependent both on the nutritional status of the individual at the time when the feathers are grown (in youth or during molt) and on the regular upkeep of the feathers. To maintain its attractive appearance, a rooster must regularly comb through its feathers with its beak or scratch with its claws to remove dust and feather mites. Research on doves has shown that the size of birds' beaks has evolved not only to rearrange feather barbs to provide a smooth appearance and protection against weather, but also to strain out the mites and other arthropods that feed on feather keratin.

Preening also helps to spread the oils from each bird's uropygial gland (near the tail) through the plumage to restore shine and to waterproof it (see page 40). However, chemists have established that in many birds the amount and types of oil in the uropygial gland secretion changes throughout the season, with more and different types of oils produced during the breeding season. Laboratory studies have demonstrated that these oils also have antibacterial properties. Rubbing oil gland secretions over the plumage not only promotes shine but also provides longer-term chemical protection against feather-degrading bacteria.

Right *Preening is essential not only to keep feathers hygienic and waterproof but also to impress social companions.*

SIGNALS OF HEALTH

The appearance of males is vital for attracting females and keeping other males at bay, but the appearance of females also matters. Social displays of plumage patterns allow individuals to recognize (and respect) higher-ranking companions in the pecking order.

In additions, hens, like roosters, benefit from appearing more vigorous, in better condition, and healthier. When mating, a rooster assesses the familiarity and condition of each of his partners and invests more resources (sperm) in hens that appear more ready to lay eggs of a better size and nutrition and provide greater care for their chicks.

Finally, both males and females benefit from appearing (and being) healthy. This is because mating represents both a benefit (fertilization) and a risk for both sexes. Sexually transmitted diseases can reduce the health of individuals and this can be manifest in a sickly, wet, poorly maintained, and patchy plumage. In essence, even feather mites and feather-degrading bacteria can be considered sexually transmitted in birds, because although hens can be quite social, there is limited physical contact with males.

GETTING DIRTY
TO KEEP CLEAN

However much chickens seek out fresh water for drinking, they do not enjoy bathing in it. Instead, dust bathing is typically performed every other day on average for both males and females. If a dry sand box is not provided for chickens, for example, they will actively create a communal dust bath themselves; they will find a corner of the backyard, rid it of vegetation, and expose the soil.

It is not immediately obvious how spreading sand and soil through the plumage can be beneficial for cleanliness and appearance. The answer lies in the fine microstructure of feathers that generates the overall appearance, shine, and subtle color of avian plumage. Oil gland secretions work to keep the sheen on and the bacteria off the feathers, but during the course of a day of foraging, fighting, and roosting, the oil also attracts dust particles and rubs off on the soil and the vegetation. Taking a dip in water would not have much effect on this oily layer because it is not soluble in water.

Instead, chickens bathe themselves in dust to soak up the oil. These oily dust particles are then more easily dislodged by using the beak to carefully comb through the plumes during the preening process, when a clean layer of oil is applied. It has also been proposed that any insects, such as ants and termites, picked up during dust bathing, might also serve a beneficial function in removing mites and ticks from the plumage and the skin of the birds.

Right *Instead of water baths, chickens strictly opt for sand to keep their feathers clean and smooth.*

LOOKING GOOD

- Remember that appearance is an important part of the way chickens interact; so make sure that they are always protected from the worst of the elements.

- Provide a sand box for use as a dust bath, or make sure that there is an area of the run that is dry enough for the same use.

- Check birds for evidence of mites and ticks and provide suitable treatment, if necessary.

Avoiding Predators

The simplest and best strategy to keep away from predators is to stay hidden. Living in the thick undergrowth of the tropical South Asian forests allows wild jungle fowl to keep hidden from the sight of many diurnal, avian predators. In turn, roosting higher up, in the canopy, at night, provides safety from the nocturnal emergence of terrestrial, mammalian predators.

In the backyard, domesticated chickens have given up some of these strategies and spend most of their days in the open, looking for grain and grubs, displaying and quarreling, dust bathing and preening. However, when it comes to night-time, all chickens still prefer to roost on a high perch in the coop or up on a tree. Similarly, chickens prefer to nest and to incubate their eggs in spots well hidden from the observing eye.

Nevertheless, when outside during the day, today's chickens still keep a watchful eye on the skies from where hawks and falcons can still attack them. Indeed, even in captivity and under carefully controlled laboratory conditions, chickens exposed to a moving image of a falconlike silhouette respond by crouching to stay hidden from the potential predator.

ALARM CALLING

Some chickens, if they spot a hawk, do not crouch or move for cover, but instead call out loud to signal the potential danger to neighboring chickens. Mother hens might be expected to do this, because it ensures that their young escape predation.

However, nonparental chickens (such as solitary hens or roosters, which provide no tangible paternal care whatsoever) also issue these alarm calls, even if it benefits other hens in the flock instead of their genetic relatives (see pages 58–59 and 72–73). Such alarm calling, nonetheless, can still be beneficial if the other flock members are also willing to call when first spotting a predator; such a tit-for-tat strategy is probably beneficial to both the individuals and flock cohesion.

Below *Scanning the sky for aerial predators is a useful survival tool for both feral and backyard chickens alike.*

MOBBING PREDATORS

If they are spotted—and see their prey alarm calling and seeking shelter—many predators will abandon their hunt and search for other prey. However, some predators, especially terrestrial ones, might decide to continue with their attack even when there is no longer the element of surprise. In these situations, flock cohesion can have yet another critical benefit for chickens, through coordinated mobbing of the predator. Predators, including minks, rats, and snakes, preying on chicks and eggs, can be successfully prevented from attacking members of the flock after having experienced the threat and physical damage of several hens' beaks and the rooster's beak and spurs.

Below *A benefit of group living is the ability to mob predators larger and more dangerous to an individual than to the whole flock.*

Alarm Calls

Alarm calls are vocalizations emitted in the presence of potential danger; among rodents and birds, alarm calls typically are given when a predator has been spotted. Although superficially such calls are clearly beneficial (adaptive), the concept behind them has long troubled behavioral ecologists and ornithologists. This is because there is no inherent benefit for a potential prey individual to make itself more vulnerable by calling loudly in the presence of a likely predator.

Some explanations for the evolution of alarm calling have assumed that these are, in fact, communication signals between the prey and the predator. By alerting the predator that it has been spotted and can no longer rely on a surprise attack, the prey is more likely to escape predation. Under this assumption, there is no cost to alarm calling and it represents honest communication where both parties benefit. The prey benefits because it is less likely to be attacked unexpectedly and the predator benefits because it will probably abandon the now obvious attack and refocus its efforts elsewhere.

Other scientists have suggested that alarm calls are communication signals to other potential prey, including the young, relatives, and other group members of social animals, to alert these partners to the presence of the predator. The cost is the increased chance of attack (and death) on the alarm caller, whereas the benefit is the reduced chance of a surprise attack

AUDIENCE EFFECTS ON ALARM CALLING IN CHICKENS

The dominant rooster benefits from being the focus of attention from hens in the backyard, but also contributes to group success and social cohesion by keeping competitor subordinate males which are being a nuisance away and calling hens to rich food sources. Aerial alarm calling by roosters also promotes group success and ensures the better survival of their young through helping female mates to escape frequent predator attacks.

Experiments have shown that an aerial alarm call is more reliably given by roosters in the presence of other chickens; the presence of hens increases calling rates, but so too does the presence or video image and sound track of unfamiliar chicks or hens. In contrast, the image of an empty cage, or a species other than chickens, such as a bobwhite quail, does not generate the same higher calling rate.

These "audience effect" results are consistent with the assumption that aerial alarm calling is costly for the rooster because it attracts the predator's attention to it; otherwise he would call irrespective of the presence of hens and chicks. It also suggests that costly vocal communication signals by a dominant male toward its group members improve all of their survival prospects, and benefit the rooster by keeping group cohesion strong and successful (see page 128).

on relatives with whom the caller shares its genes. Other benefits may include greater participation by unrelated group members in reciprocal alarm calling (tit-for-tat), contributing to group cohesion and social bonding, or the signaling of prowess and high status by the caller ("Look, I can call, save you, AND escape predation!"—termed the "handicap principle" by Israeli scientist A. Zahavi).

These types of benefits can only accrue in the kind of tightly structured group living that chickens demonstrate. Chickens have, therefore, become popular and productive subjects for the study of the function and content of alarm calling behaviors and signals.

Flock Formation

Taking home a single chick from a country fair or a breeders' competition may seem like a great way to let children observe the biological realities of growing up, but a single chick is unlikely to lead a fulfilled life, unless it is fully adopted into the family structure of its hosts.

Chickens are a social species, and their behaviors have been carefully shaped by millennia of natural and artificial selection to perform successfully in a social, group setting.

The most important aspect of a chicken flock is the stability of its structure: this can be helped by a single dominant rooster and a linear hierarchy, i.e. a carefully established pecking order among the hens (see pages 138–139).

Social cohesion is essential for everyday functions of the flock, such as discovering and sharing foods, staying alert and escaping from predators, and accessing mates and alliances for breeding and social status quo.

Above *Chickens are happiest and healthiest when living in tight -knit groups.*

Right *Hens form a highly structured hierarchy within the flock led by the alpha chicken (which is a hen, not a rooster!).*

Behavioral and psychological aspects of flock cohesion involve the formation of long-term memories of individuals (the rooster, the higher-up members of the pecking order, own chicks, etc.), and discriminating familiar individuals from newcomers, cooperators from selfish actors, and aggressors from subordinates; these cognitive abilities imply a detailed representation of individual and social complexities in each chicken's brain and cognitive architecture (see page 136).

Despite the importance of social cohesion, the chicken flock is anything but a peaceful society (see page 78–81). The established hierarchy among the hens is constantly challenged by subordinates looking to compete and win against more dominant hens. More dominant individuals benefit from accessing food and water more quickly, by taking higher perches for the night roosts in the coop, and, in general, by being harassed and pecked less often, including attacks from several more dominant individuals against a lower status female.

Similarly, the dominant rooster is constantly challenged by satellite males sneaking into the flock to forcefully mate with hens or directly compete and fight with the resident male. Females pay close attention to the rooster's ability to maintain its dominance; a rooster who suffers repeated challenges and fails to prevail against intruders can occasionally be attacked by groups of females. But, both flock cohesion and challenges to it are necessary to make sure of the continued success of the flock.

Individuals whose condition deteriorates or is impacted by diseases can no longer provide essential cooperative behaviors for the flock: alerting others to predators in time for the whole flock to escape, calling others to share a rich find of food, and protecting the next brood of chicks from weather and other dangers.

Policing of the condition, status, and health of flock members by each other ensures reciprocal benefits to the selfish interests of the individuals and the better survival of related flock members to pass on shared genes to the next generations.

The social hierarchies in the chicken flock must have sufficient flexibility and malleability to adjust to its ever-changing composition; with each successful hatching, a new brood of initially unfamiliar chicks will start to seek their positions in the well-established pecking order of the flock. Also, in the wild and in captivity, individual flock members are subject to attacks by predators (or being used for a nice dinner in their keepers' household), which means that dominant and subordinate flock members might disappear from one day to the next; the flock order must continually allow for dynamic readjustment.

SOCIAL FUNCTIONS & COSTS OF FLOCKS

In the wild, flocks of fowl provide collective access to food and safe roosting sites, protection from predators and competitors, and cooperation between familiar and often related group members.

Many of these functions are no longer necessary in captive flocks of chickens. In backyards and other forms of low-density housing, several of the original flock structures continue to persist. These include dominance hierarchies established among the hens, displays and fights among roosters to yield a single dominant male, and alarm and food calling in response to predators and rich food finds.

Chickens housed in cages or in large-scale industrial settings display only a few remnants of ancestral flock structure—often with highly detrimental outcomes. If chickens are held in such high numbers that they rarely become familiar with each other—or cage-composition is constantly rotated—physical displays and fights involved in establishing and maintaining dominance hierarchies are actually no longer meaningful.

Nevertheless, pecks to probe and police the pecking order are still delivered, causing severe wounds and even fatalities. Similarly, group cohesion may be manifest through the formation of temporary alliances to attack injured or otherwise vulnerable individuals, again often resulting in death and even cannibalism.

It is also possible that in large-scale industrial breeding situations, individuals are more selfish and less flock oriented, so that any self-policing to stop the pecking of subordinate and weak individuals once dominance has been established is lost, which results in further injury and death in the cage and on the floor of the chicken farm.

FLOCK CARE

- Always think carefully before introducing new chickens to a flock and watch out for adverse reactions.

- Remember that an individual hen can recognize up to ninety six other individuals. Keeping flock sizes well below this number allows for a stable social hierarchy.

- Bear in mind that the flock size will grow with every new hatching.

Right *Chickens keep many of their social behaviors, both the affiliative and aggressive ones, in large enclosures as if they were still living in small flocks.*

Aggression, Competition, & Alliances

Most animals exhibit different behavior when faced with familiar and unfamiliar individuals of their own species, and with individuals of a different species—demonstrating an ability to tell such individuals apart. In species where social groups form the core of daily life, including many fowl species, such social recognition systems are even more sophisticated. For example, Japanese quail are able to use facial markings of never-before-seen individuals to tell related and unrelated individuals apart; this ability to recognize relatives (kin) is beneficial because it allows the quail to avoid mating with too-closely related individuals and avoid the costs of inbreeding.

When it comes to choice of mate, kin recognition is about avoiding related individuals instead of approaching them. However, in flock formation the same ability is also used to establish alliances between kin, the structure and duration of which last longer than groups formed by unrelated individuals.

This is because related chickens are more likely to stick to the principles of cooperation and reciprocity on which group cohesion relies. By issuing an alarm call when they spot a predator or sharing the location of a pile of grain or grubs, chickens in kin groups enhance the survival of closely related individuals, who themselves carry a larger

Below *A newcomer needs to establish her role in the flock quickly to start building alliances.*

than background share of similar genes. Moreover, these shared genes would better propagate through time, enhancing cooperation and group cohesion further.

In the short term, selfish chickens might benefit more from group membership than altruistic individuals who call about predators and food. Such individuals would gain better condition and leave more offspring behind, but these offspring themselves would be more selfish. Therefore, over time, the level of cooperation would break down and the flock would dissolve.

Predicting social behaviors, therefore, is strongly dependent on context, and careful scientists and observant natural historians can recognize these different stages of social complexity easily.

COMPETITION WITHIN FLOCKS

A paradoxical outcome of strong group cohesion and stable flock formation is that levels of competition may be higher in groups composed of some relatives compared to groups of unrelated individuals. This is because relatives already share a fair amount of genetic material. Accordingly, even if one individual out-competes another for food, matings, and other resources, the progeny of that successful individual will still share some genes with the loser of the initial contest. Thus, losing in a competition among related individuals might still generate more benefits (more offspring produced with shared genes) than sharing resources equitably in a group of unrelated individuals.

A classic example of asymmetrical sharing between members of a strongly cohesive group has been provided by the genetic analysis of the relatedness and siring success of a close relative of chickens, the wild turkey. Here, young males from the same brood, typically full brothers, will remain together for many years after reaching independence; group membership is beneficial because of the increased vigilance of larger flocks of brothers against predators.

Also, when the breeding season arrives, groups composed of more male turkeys have greater success in catching the attention of females, who seek out males only to fertilize the eggs—much like in chickens.

Still, in a flock of male turkeys, only a single male ever mates with the females, all the others (his brothers) stay behind and do not contribute genetic materials to the next generation. Solitary males are occasionally successful, but sire many fewer young than the alpha males in groups.

Nonetheless, it might be thought that siring a handful of young is still more beneficial than siring none (as is done by beta and gamma males in groups). This is, however, not the case, because the genes shared between brothers outweigh the cost of not siring chicks directly. As a result, male coalitions in turkeys are stable because individuals benefit either directly or indirectly through passing on more genes (including those involved in the behavioral and cognitive basis of coalition formation) into the next generation.

AGGRESSION WITHIN FLOCKS

Maintaining the social hierarchy of a well-structured flock, including the dominant status of the resident rooster and the pecking order among the hens, requires intensive bouts of dynamic assessment of the competitive abilities, potential, and skills of each contestant.

Even when the hierarchy is established, it is constantly probed and policed by minor behavioral and physical confrontations between the differently ranked individuals (see page 136).

A recent study set out to determine whether continued fighting is the necessary outcome of establishing a dominance hierarchy, or a detrimental distraction caused by individuals challenging the status quo.

Researchers observed a group of hens to establish their original pecking order and then gave flock members hormone injections of testosterone (the male aggression hormone known to increase aggression in females, too). As predicted, the intensity of the fights increased between group members. Contrary to expectations, however, group structure and pecking order showed little change following the hormone injections.

These results suggest that cognitive skills to recognize more or less dominant and subordinate individuals play a strong role in maintaining group cohesion in chicken flocks, and the occasional fights observed under unmanipulated (natural) conditions in the backyard do not significantly destabilize flock structure and function.

Right *Roosters fight to display their skills and potential abilities, and determine their status, which is important in maintaining the stability of the flock.*

Calling & Other Vocalizations ～⌇

Humans are undoubtedly a unique biological species and possess genetic, anatomical, and physiological features not shared with any other organisms. However, animal behaviorists, psychologists, and philosophers have also long debated whether any of the individual behavioral or cognitive traits displayed by humans are uniquely distinct from those of the rest of the animals.

Language, for example, is defined as the rule-base use of arbitrary communication signals to denote infinite meaning. This begs the question of whether animals have language similar to ours. This question can be best answered by breaking it down to its core constituents. For example, do animals have the ability to learn language much like children have the ability to learn to speak their mother tongue? In addition, do some species of animals have their own set of arbitrary communication signals, which are combined according to a specified set of rules (syntax)? And finally, do communication signals of animals denote a particular meaning in an arbitrary manner?

Birds have been identified by scientists as a suitable subject for experimental

Left *Communication and self-advertisement are both achieved by the rooster's crow.*

analysis of language-like learning and motor patterns; parrots and starlings can easily learn the words of human speech and some individuals are able to combine these words and communicate meaning.

More relevant, perhaps, is that the songs of warblers and larks are learned by mimicking tutors, much like children learn human languages; such songs are used to communicate the presence, status, and intent of the singer, similar to speech and writing based on language; and, finally, the production and perception of these songs requires specialized brain areas in the telencephalon, similar to the areas dedicated to language in the brains of humans.

Thus, birdsong is languagelike in both its function and structure, as well as in its neural and cognitive mechanisms. But do song notes and syllables denote a clearly identifiable meaning similar to words and modifiers in human language?

MEANING IN CALLING?

Surprisingly, advances in our knowledge about the potential paths and trajectories of language evolution in nonhuman animals come from species that do not learn their vocalizations by mimicking their parents or other tutors, including chickens. For example, vervet monkeys in the African savanna do not mimic the calls of other individuals but still use three different alarm calls to warn of the approach of hawks, snakes, and leopards.

At least two of these alarm calls do not sound to the human ear like the vocalizations or noises produced by the predators (except for the leopard alarm call which is a felinelike bark). When researchers played back the sounds of these calls in the absence of the predators, the vervet monkeys responded as if they had spotted the predator; in response to the snake alarm call, they stood up and surveyed the ground, and in response to the eagle alarm call, they looked up and hid under the canopy of a tree. Thus, these calls denote specific and arbitrary meaning to the vervet monkeys.

REFERENTIAL CALLS
IN CHICKENS

Extensive research into the vocal repertoire of chickens has also revealed the presence and use of referential calls by both hens and roosters. This implies a species-level ability to both produce and decode the meaning of referential calls across the sexes in chickens (see page 128).

Roosters, for example, will call to hens in the flock after discovering a pile of grains or finding earthworms in the soil. Similarly, mother hens produce food calls to attract their chicks to share the finds. These calls are arbitrary in structure in that they neither resemble the sounds made by grubs, earthworms, or other food items, nor do they sound like a rooster or a hen consuming these food items.

Playback of these calls, in the absence of the rooster or the mother hen, causes a strong response; hens and chicks will approach the sound source, with many of the responders looking and pecking at the ground nearby as if searching for food.

Similarly, the aerial alarm call of chickens does not sound like either the high-pitch whines of hawks or falcons, or the sound of escaping chickens; thus they represent an arbitrary communication signal. In turn, playback of the call, in the absence of both the caller and the raptor's image, evokes responses of crouching and looking upward in other chickens; thus, the call represents a referential signal carrying a specific function.

Are such referential calls evidence of language in chickens? Not at all. At best, they represent protolanguage through arbitrary signal design universally denoting a specific meaning. What remains to be examined experimentally is whether these chicken calls can be or are routinely combined according to a universal set of rules.

Whether such combinations can be used to generate a more complex and novel meaning remains a question still to be answered by scientists. In other words, could these signals be part of true language?

Left *Roosters use referential calls to signal to hens of the discovery of food.*

Right *Young chicks are quick to respond and to produce specific calls to recognize relatives and to hide from predators.*

The Consequences of Mating ~

WHAT FEMALES WANT (& DO NOT WANT)

Although not essential, hens benefit greatly and directly from being associated with a dominant and healthy rooster; he is more likely to find and share food with them and to keep away subordinate males from the flock. In addition, because many of the visual, vocal, cognitive, healthy, and other behavioral displays and traits of a rooster will probably be in part controlled by his genetic makeup, mating with the dominant rooster assures that females will receive and use his superior genetic material to fertilize their own eggs and pass these traits on to the next generation.

Although the size and sex composition of flocks in most captive situations is well controlled, in feral fowl populations, subordinate roosters often force themselves onto females and copulate without big courtship displays or clear signs of female receptivity. Such a scenario of forced copulations is present in many wild bird species, from bank swallows to Australasian gannets, and will probably have been present in ancestral jungle-fowl populations. This is suspected to be the case because studies have revealed

that hens in feral chicken populations have sophisticated sperm management strategies so that they can rid themselves of potentially lower quality and poorer composition sperm after having been forced to mate by a subordinate male.

In contrast, when given a free choice, females seek to mate with socially more dominant males and those that display larger fleshy combs. If the males are matched up for size and appearance, receptive females choose to spend time with those males that flap their wings more often than nearby competitors.

Below *Hens choose males based on a very specific set of criteria, which are often shared between the different females.*

Above *Mating in birds is quick, appears awkward and uncomfortable, and can result in some pulled feathers and peck marks.*

WHAT MALES WANT (& DO NOT WANT)

Despite popular belief, copulation and provision of sperm both have potential dangers and costs. Although copulations in birds are typically short in duration, they still, for example, expose the copulating pair to attack from competitors and predators. Moreover, there is evidence that sexually transmitted parasites and other diseases may be abundant in commercially kept birds and are generally present in wild species, too.

This may explain some of the unexpected mating strategies of individuals and populations that deviate from the typical rules of mating decisions. This is known as the Bateman paradigm, which declares females to be choosy when mating with males and males to be willing to mate with most females (see page 61).

Even in those species, such as chickens, where males avidly compete for access to receptive females, and most males lose out by not mating even once in their lives, many of the dominant, successful males engage in their own strategy of mate choice and sperm management.

Specifically, roosters invest more time and transfer more sperm to females that are novel and unfamiliar to the mating context or to females that display flashier and brighter combs, the color of which indicates greater egg-laying ability and better skills at incubating the eggs and raising the chicks successfully.

This careful, beneficial, and strategic manipulation in roosters' mating tactics with females is consistent with the costly sperm hypothesis. However, it still makes

individuals more prone to carry sexually transmitted diseases, which need to be monitored in captive populations.

WHAT CHICKS WANT

In all sexually reproducing species, the genetic contributions of females and males combine to generate new life and new individuals: chicks are not exact replicas of their parents but a unique mix of their parents' genes.

Roosters, on the one hand, contribute through genetic materials provided to fertilize the egg. They also provide warning of predators and protection from subordinate males, and give the mother hen access to some food sources, thereby directly enhancing her chances of safety, survival, nourishment, and successful reproduction.

Females, on the other hand, provide a genetic contribution to the chick, and invest heavily into nourishing the lipid-, vitamin-, and hormone-rich yolk, the antibacterial enzymes of the albumin, and the strong yet porous calcium-base eggshell.

Above *Chicks benefit both from the care of the hen and from being part of a large brood of chicks, which reduces the chance of being picked out by a predator.*

Right *Each chick represents a genetic experiment of mixing up half of each parent's genes in a never-before-tried combination.*

Yet, because of the fundamental genetic relationship between males, females, and their chicks, there is conflict between the long-term interests of individual chicks among themselves and with their mother, because all of them, on average, only share 50 percent of their genes with others. Selfishness is natural, so it can only be expected that individual chicks act to increase their own survival over those of their brood mates.

Chicks run to be the first to pick up a food item, push deeper inside the plumage of the mother hen during bouts of brooding, and keep the shortest distance from her to return to the safety of the mother after an alarm call; these are all indications that chicks are selfish in relation to other chicks and, hence, cause conflict with their mother whose own goal is to provide equitable care for each chick.

However, cooperation among chicks is also present in the brood before and after hatching: older embryos, for example, call to each other in the last few days inside the egg to coordinate the timing of hatching and departure from the nest.

Cooperation in the face of selfishness can have at least three different types of positive outcome:
1.) mutual sharing of the benefit; all chicks benefit from hatching together and moving away from the nest as a group, due to safety in numbers;
2.) reciprocal benefits, where benefits are provided and received sequentially by different individuals so that, over time, each gain equally;
3.) kin-selected benefits, whereby acts of altruism are truly costly to the individual but the benefit is that the individual's close relatives (siblings, with whom it shares 50 percent of genes) may survive longer and carry those shared genes to be passed on into the next generation.

Nest Building & Egg Laying

Without strong powered flight, but sporting plumage that blends well into the background of the forest floor, fowls unsurprisingly typically nest on the ground. Most female birds lay a single egg each day during the laying period, followed by incubation, hatching, and looking after the young, whether helped by the male or not.

Precocial bird species, whose young hatch fully downed and ready to leave the nest on their own within a day, typically lay more eggs than altricial (nest-dwelling) species. Their eggs are also usually larger and take longer to incubate. This means that the nest is more exposed to predation during the extensive laying period both because it takes more days to lay a full clutch and because the hen typically does not start incubation until the clutch is completed, so that the eggs will hatch synchronously and the chicks can be led away from the nest all together.

Yet, predation is the leading source of nest failure in wild birds, so we can expect that different avian species have evolved

Left *Hens provide the best microclimate for incubating eggs: intense warmth and high humidity.*

specific behaviors to accommodate high rates of predation. For fowls, including chickens, this is manifest in the quick and superficial nest building behaviors of the hens; they scrape a shallow depression into the soil and pull grass stems and other plant materials to line the nest.

Such a nest is easy and fast to replace and will not delay the ability to initiate renesting by the hen, should her nest site be found and the eggs be eaten or lost.

AN EGG A DAY

From ovulation through fertilization to the formation and pigmentation of the calcite eggshell (a crystalline form of calcium carbonate, distinct from limestone), the ovum takes about a full day to travel through the oviduct to the cloaca and, eventually, into the nest.

Although most female bird embryos have two ovaries, mature females typically have one functional ovary (on the left), so that only one egg can be produced at most in each 24-hour period (see pages 36–37). In addition, the female requires extra resources, namely rich foods, to generate enough lipids, vitamins, and hormones to deposit into the egg yolk and to generate diverse enzymes with antibacterial properties for the albumin to protect the embryo from pathogens.

The calcareous eggshell itself is also costly to produce; after the first or second egg, internal calcium storages in the bones are depleted by laying birds and additional calcium-rich foods must be eaten to make a strong eggshell to last until hatching.

Finally, most strains of chickens deposit distinct compositions of two colorful pigments on the outmost layer of the eggshell, consisting of biliverdin (which generates blue-green hues) and protoporphyrin (rusty red hues; also responsible for the speckles in those species of birds that lay maculated eggs). Both of these pigments require specific biochemical machinery in the female because they are generated anew at the shell gland of the hen, and they are metabolic derivatives of the blood's oxygen-carrying hemoglobin molecules and related in structure to the colorful bile pigments of mammals.

CALCIUM BOOST

- Provide laying hens with a calcium-rich diet such as ground-up oyster shells to help with the production of eggshells and ward off calcium depletion in the bones.

Incubation

It is fair to say that, with industrial-scale breeding operations all around the world, most chickens alive today will have been hatched in an incubator. But in feral populations and in many backyards, natural incubation and maternal care are still the standard.

The wild ancestors of chickens typically lay 8–12 eggs, which is a large clutch size for a relatively small bird species, even if it is precocial. From the onset of incubation, only the females engage in the various tasks of keeping the eggs and chicks warm, safe, and dry and leading the hatchlings to food and safety.

Domesticated chickens can easily incubate 12–16 eggs, with hens of larger varieties able to hatch twenty. Some breeders use foster parents, such as turkeys or ducks, to incubate and hatch valuable eggs of highly prized strains that have poor maternal instincts; most of these methods of using live females to incubate

eggs generate a higher success rate (more than 90 percent) than artificial incubation with automated egg rotators (80 to 90 percent) or hand rotation (50 percent).

GOING BROODY

Female chickens readily lay eggs in communal nests and share the space with other laying hens. However, after producing 10–12 eggs, some females dramatically change their behaviors and become secretive, immobile, and strongly attached to a particular nesting box. If another female has also laid in the same location, both females might share to incubate the same clutch, typically with poor success.

A brooding female is easily identified by its attachment to the clutch, the lack of motivation to leave, even when handled, and uncharacteristically aggressive calling and pecking, instead of escaping,

Below Most of the billions of chickens alive today are hatched in industrial incubators.

Domestication and extensive artificial incubation have caused many strains of chickens to display reduced broodiness— or even none at all. For instance, an incubating female sitting on a nest in a busy corner of the coop might perceive the disturbance as signs of imminent predation and opt to abandon the breeding attempt in search of safer sites.

Alternatively, the timing of the broodiness may have been disconnected from the actual duration of the required incubation period, and females intensively incubating for two weeks might abandon their well-developing and fully viable eggs laid into a safe nest site.

In these cases, breeders should be ready to move the eggs into an already running incubator, or transfer them into the nest of a recently broody female. Viable eggs nearer to hatching are more valuable both biologically and economically than freshly laid ones.

Above *Once incubation has been begun by the broody hen, she rarely leaves the eggs unattended.*

when approached and handled by their keepers. Some females will also drop some feathers and develop a naked patch of skin on their belly—the brood patch, which is rich in blood vessels and suitable for transferring more heat to the eggs more efficiently. By staying closely on the nest, and only leaving it once a day to feed, drink, defecate, and dust bathe, the broody hen draws minimal attention to the nest site, covers the eggs with her own cryptic plumage for most hours of the day, protects the eggs from small rodent predators, and provides a warm and humid microclimate for the eggs.

CARE OF BROODY HENS

- Watch out for signs of broodiness, such as attachment to, and defense of, the clutch.

- Be vigilant for abandoned nest sites; be ready to move eggs to an incubator or another occupied nest.

- Provide plenty of possible nesting sites to minimize the possibility of competition.

Behavior of Embryos

A chicken embryo starts its life in a solid hard cave, made up from the same chemical material (calcite) as limestone (calcium carbonate), from which there is no clear exit or escape hole. The light might shine through the cave's wall occasionally, but most of the time there is complete darkness.

The cave is too tight for the embryo to move around freely, let alone stretch its legs and wings, and air is supplied for breathing by a small bubble near the tip of the egg. It is no small wonder then that when the time comes, after about three weeks, hatching is initiated and accomplished so efficiently.

BEHAVIOR BEFORE HATCHING

The last few days of life within the eggshell are critical for the successful development of the embryo. There is intensive calling between the incubating hen and the unhatched young, as well as between the embryos.

Hearing the calls allows mother and young to recognize and establish the mother–offspring bond at the time of hatching without ever having seen each

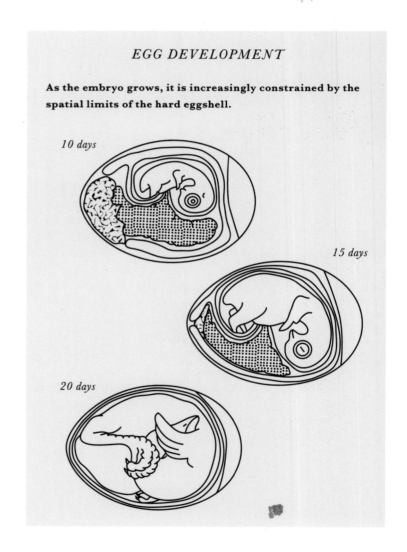

EGG DEVELOPMENT

As the embryo grows, it is increasingly constrained by the spatial limits of the hard eggshell.

10 days

15 days

20 days

other before. Similarly, hearing others in neighboring eggs in the nest synchronizes the time at which the chicks complete their last stages of development and come to hatch; this so-called hatching synchrony, or the simultaneous hatching of eggs in the same clutch, is highly beneficial to precocial birds, including chickens, whose young depart the nest together after leaving the egg.

This is because any unhatched young are inevitably left behind without the protection or brooding of the mother while she leads the hatchlings away from the nest toward food and safety.

GETTING READY FOR THE WORLD OUTSIDE THE EGG

There is a surprising benefit to being packed tightly within the egg in the days just before the chick hatches. The lack of space prevents extensive movement, so the nearly fully grown embryo receives external stimuli, including light, asymmetrically. In particular, its right eye

is positioned toward the eggshell but its left eye is covered by the rest of its torso. This means that only the right eye is exposed to light filtered through the shell when the hen is away from the nest and her duties of incubation (see page 119).

This initial asymmetry translates into asymmetrical sensory and neural processing of visual stimuli by the hatchling chick, including its preference to use its right eye to peck at pebbles and grains when searching for food. Such "lateralization" is essentially the same as human handedness, and is common among birds.

The benefit of using paired sensory organs, and the underlying brain structures, in such a lateralized manner is that even the young chick's brain is able to process complex and multiple sets of stimuli: using the right eye for feeding, and using the left eye to spot hawks and other predators.

Scientists have shown, by keeping eggs in total darkness, that light exposure of just six hours during the last three days before hatching is enough to establish this strong sidedness in the behavior of chicks; it can also be reversed by exposing only the left eye to light before hatching.

So the next time you see chicks out and about, watch whether they tilt their head to the right before pulling on a tasty blade of grass or stare at you with their left eye before running back to their protective mother hen.

Below Hatchling chicks are quick to get on their feet and to seek out the mother hen, warmth, and food.

Hatching ～

The domestic chick embryo spends twenty one days inside the egg once incubation has begun. This is two days longer than the incubation period of the wild red jungle fowl, perhaps because the domestic egg is larger and relatively better supplied with yolk.

Still, once the three weeks are up, the chicks are faced with the gravest of their tasks yet: to hatch from the solid calcium-crystal-walled cave that is the hard-shelled egg. To be fair, the thickness and porosity of the calcite eggshell changes during incubation; the shell becomes thinner and the pores become larger as the embryo harnesses the calcium in the shell to build its own endoskeleton.

SYNCHRONIZATION OF HATCHING

Hatching is synchronized between the different eggs in the brood; this is achieved both by the delayed onset of incubation by the broody hen, near clutch completion, and the vocal communication of the chicks peeping to each other at around three days before hatching.

This typically allows slow-developing embryos to speed up growth and maturation and results in their hatching within 24 hours of the rest of the clutch. Around three days before hatching is also

Below *Hatching is hard physical labor, but its result is freedom to actively seek out nutrients, heat, and safety.*

when the female stops rotating her eggs in the nest; not rotating the eggs prior to that in artificial incubators causes developmental deformities, while rotating eggs after that interferes with the chick's ability to hatch.

The success of hatching, therefore, depends on the rate and consistency of early egg rotation, but it is also affected by the high humidity levels in artificial incubators. High humidity mimics the microclimate of the chicken nest, generated by its plant material-base lining, the gas exchange of the many eggs in the nest, and the insulation to seal in the warmth and humidity underneath the mother hen's plumage sitting on the eggs.

HATCHING TIME

About a day before hatching, a small opening appears near the large (blunt end) of the chicken egg. This is made by the sharp keratinized egg tooth of the embryo, positioned on the top mandible and lost soon after hatching. The embryo continues to peep, further coordinating the timing of hatching with the rest of the clutch. It also frequently rotates and pushes itself around the inside of the eggshell to generate a circular cut at the blunt pole. This is high-intensity physical work, so the chick takes frequent breaks, all the while continuing to call.

Eventually, the chick breaks the shell into two asymmetrical pieces and the embryo pushes its head through the hole, followed by its wet body. It continues its peep calls in response to the mother hen's clucks and the peeps of the other chicks and eggs, often positioning itself against another hatching egg, and, under "natural" conditions, warmed under the brooding mother hen.

For nourishment, the young chick relies on the yolk sac's lipid storage, which it absorbed just before hatching. About a day later, together with the other successfully hatched young, it departs from the nest, led by the mother hen to food, water, and safety.

Parental Behavior

Biologists maintain a strict conceptual difference between "parental care" and "parental investment." Parental care is defined as the provisioning and protective behaviors to support the survival and success of dependent young by the parents.

Parental investment is defined as those behaviors that provide for the young but that require a significant cost—reducing the chance for survival and future reproduction by the parents.

All avian progeny require parental care in the form of heat provided to begin incubation. Including the various strategies by which different species warm their eggs, the types and costs of parental care vary widely across bird species.

MATERNAL CARE

In chickens, males are said not to provide any paternal care, because roosters take no part in the nest building, incubation, and chick-raising steps of looking after the next generation.

In turn, females pay a heavy set of costs, including the provision of lipids and calcium for the egg, building the nest and incubating the eggs in it, brooding and leading the chicks to food and safety, and then repeating the full cycle again and again.

Maternal care in chickens increases the ability of the young to remain hidden from predators and to learn about suitable food items. However, it also reduces the lifespan of the mother hen, not least by diverting resources from her own nourishment, making her less capable of escaping predators and fighting pathogens.

Hens also pay several behavioral costs for motherhood. For example, incubation requires spending most hours of the day and all night on a terrestrial spot, without being able to roost on a high perch for safety. Even with a carefully hidden nest and the

camouflage afforded by her rusty feather colors, the hen is extremely vulnerable to predators during this time. She must remain stationary for long periods, and whenever she does go off to feed, drink, or dust bathe, she is laying scent trails to and from her nest—easily followed by a scent-oriented mammalian predator.

Similarly, once the chicks hatch, the mother hen continues to spend little time looking after herself. Instead, she calls around for the chicks, leads them across the yard to new sources of food, guides them away from aggressive fights by other chickens, helps them hide from aerial predators, and, while the chicks are unable to fly, ushers them back to the nest for the night. When she encounters food, the mother calls her young so that they can have first access to it. And when a predator approaches, she uses a different call to alert her young to hide or to run back to her, and protects them with her own body, if necessary.

Finally, by becoming broody and incubating the eggs to hatch and raise the young, she also forgoes the chances of continuing to lay additional eggs and thereby increase her reproductive success.

It is not surprising therefore that those hens which successfully incubate the eggs and raise the chicks will require and benefit from a period of rest away from the demanding duties of reproduction.

Below *The male provides indirect parental care by protecting all members of the flock, including the chicks he sired and their mothers.*

PATERNAL CARE

What, if any, parental role falls upon the rooster who sires many if not all of the chicks in a backyard? None of the costs of the direct investments into the chicks are borne by the male. However, the rooster's leadership and sentinel roles in the flock indirectly benefit the mother hen and her progeny. For instance, when the rooster discovers a pile of grain or several earthworms while foraging, he delivers a food call to attract the hens nearby to share the food source within the flock.

Similarly, when the rooster spots a fast-flying falcon in the sky, he is more likely to call when hens are around to alert them to the imminent danger. If the hens are also caring for chicks at the time, these young, too, benefit from being called to food and alerted to danger.

The result is that the flock maintains its structure, composition, safety, and nourishment, and the hens, as well as the rooster, communally and individually benefit through increased longevity and greater breeding success.

PARENTS & OTHER ROLE MODELS

Chicks are equipped with the skills—and organs—to hatch successfully from the egg, become fully mobile, and feed themselves within a matter of hours. Nevertheless, many aspects of a chick's behavioral repertoire and abilities are learned by observing suitable role models, i.e. both of their parents. The mother hen, naturally, serves as the model for feeding, drinking, running to safety, and keeping warm at night, while developing male chicks learn from the resident rooster about courtship, competition, and vigilance (see pages 132–133).

Other adults also act as role models, helping to fine tune the behavioral skills of the chicks, especially when it comes to fitting into the highly structured social hierarchy and performing the complex daily rituals of feeding, dust bathing, and interacting among flock members.

Viewing and memorizing the range and types of other chickens is critical for growing chicks to be able to identify their own species for mating, flock formation, and cooperation. For example, if a young rooster is cast out of its natal (birth) flock, it will need to locate another flock, perhaps without a resident male, to join and become the dominant rooster. Or young hens may get together and leave the aggressive, highly structured natal flock to start a new group, composed of other individuals of their own species. Such successful social skills depend on the ability of chicks to learn and recognize the size, color, call, and other variations in the appearance and behavior of chickens.

Behavior of Chicks

Hatching out of the hard-shelled eggs is one of the most demanding and dangerous times in any bird's life. The shell is built to be strong, and when it breaks to release the embryo, its sharp edges and bright internal layers can easily harm the hatchling and attract predators.

Although chickens are fully precocial, and the young hatch completely covered in down, they still need some time to dry up, gather their strength, find their balance, and imprint on a mother to follow for the next several weeks (see pages 122–125). To ensure that the maximum possible number of chicks are dried up and ready to leave the nest at the same time, chicks communicate through their peeps to other embryos.

Chicks do not need to feed on the first day after hatching because they can survive on the egg yolk absorbed before they hatched. However, these resources are soon depleted and the mother hen becomes increasingly anxious to lead the chicks to food and water. Those that are still wet, halfway out of the egg, or have not yet broken through are left behind, and, without the brooding heat of the hen, they are soon faced with hypothermia and die or fall prey to predators.

Until the chicks become volant (flighted) using their fast-growing wing feathers, the mother hen still returns with them to the nest during bouts of cold, rainy weather, and at night. Alternatively, she may find another suitable hidden ground location for brooding.

GROWING UP

Chicks develop fast and become more and more independent in finding food and water, locating dust bowls for bathing, avoiding the elements, and steering clear of aggressive flock members. Their wing feathers start to grow and, for a time, they sport an awkward combination of downy chick plumage and juvenile feather coverage. From about three to four weeks of age, secondary sexual characteristics, including the comb, start to develop.

This allows the keeper to tell male and female chicks apart, often to the detriment of the males. If they are not to be kept for their meat, breeding, exhibition, or sale, males at this stage may be caught and removed to save on feeding costs. The young hens go on to seek out their own food and start to make longer and more daring trips away from the mother hen. Eventually, they become fully feathered young females ready to join the flock and seek out their own position in the pecking order.

To grow successfully, chicks need access to plenty of warmth, dryness, food, water, and also grit (like adults, they use this grit to help grind down food items in their muscular gizzards, instead of using their feet or beaks to first tear up the food). Complete starter diets are designed to provide all the nutrition required by developing chicks, so many keepers and breeders recommend that supplemental feeding is not required.

But, if chicks are kept as pets or in small groups, giving them tasty morsels (grubs, fresh lettuce, young corn) can help them to establish long-lasting bonds with their keepers; they will show preferences toward someone from whom such morsels can be reliably sourced (see page 127).

CARING FOR CHICKS

- Make sure that chicks have warmth, dryness, food, water, and grit.

- If in doubt, use a commercial complete starter diet designed for developing chicks.

- Remember that chicks can recognize individual keepers; providing them with additional tasty morsels can help establish long-lasting bonds.

- Chickens reach sexual maturity at five to six months. Be sure to remove any young roosters from the flock to limit competition over breeding or unwanted fertilized eggs.

Growing chicks spend most of the daytime learning from the mother hen, the rest of their brood, the flock, and others around. However, the speed of their growth is also a drain on their energy, so chicks take frequent breaks to lie down and rest.

Sleeping chicks often lack the well-composed body posture of sleeping adults; to the untrained eye, a chick lying flat out on the bottom of a pen, with its head thrust forward and its wings spread to the sides, may appear to be dead instead of sleeping.

With time, developing young learn not to rest out in the open, instead leaning against rocks and plants, or hiding under vegetation. At about a month of age, they will vigorously flap their wings to roost on a high perch or tree branch.

Sleeping is also essential for the developing young because it allows the brain quiet time in which to recruit more neurons and build the complex connections and architecture needed to form long-lasting memories.

This process in itself represents an even greater drain on a young chicken's energy; neuronal tissues use up more energy than any other organ in the body, so the growing brain requires even more nourishment from one day to the next.

REACHING ADULTHOOD

If they survive hatching, drying up, the occasional misstep and crowding under the brooding hen, attacks by hungry predators, and the possibility of infection, young chicks reach adulthood typically at five to six months of age. At this point, young hens start to lay and young roosters produce viable sperm, although in a backyard or feral setting the older males make sure that mating by these youngsters is kept at a minimum.

Whether they remain with their natal flock, join a different one, or even establish a new one of their own, newly adult hens face a period as challenging as anything they have experienced so far. In the next few months of life, they must learn how to live and survive on their own and use whatever life skills they have picked up to fit into a new social hierarchy.

Right *Competition with each other is in the nature of all adult roosters, whether young or mature, and whether related to each other or strangers.*

Behavioral Role Models

Many of the behaviors that we associate with chickens appear to be present from day one after hatching. Hatchling chicks, for example, peck on insects and grains, look up toward a fast-flying object, and keep to close quarters with other chickens.

Some developmental scientists have termed such behaviors instinctual or innate, but if we start looking early enough, we can see that these behaviors are learned. For example, if small umbrellas are placed around the feet of hatchlings, the chicks will fail to develop an interest in pecking at worms and grubs. This is because the initial impetus for reaching out for long thin objects comes from pecking at their own toe; the umbrellas hide the toes and delay the onset of directed pecking behavior.

LEARNING FROM MOTHER HEN

The life of a hatchling chick depends fully on the protection and care provided by the mother hen; roosters have no interest in provisioning young, whereas hens freshly done with the chores of incubation face several more weeks of providing chicks with heat and protection from the elements, defending them from predators and other risks, leading them to food and water, and guiding them away from novel and potentially dangerous places and objects. Thus, establishing the bond between chick and hen—known as filial imprinting—is critical (see page 123).

Chicks in the laboratory readily imprint on all types of objects, but those that move, that make sounds, and that approach the hatchling chick are more likely to be the focus of imprinting than inanimate and silent objects.

Both the timing and the sensory stimuli involved in filial imprinting are allocated to and controlled by specific brain areas in the young chick. This makes the young chick a suitable and popular study subject for experimental analysis of the neural basis of sensitive periods and of learning and memory in general.

LEARNING FROM OTHERS

Mother hens cannot individually provide all the visual, vocal, tactile, and behavioral stimuli needed for a chick to learn properly how to behave as a socially successful member of the chicken flock. Male chicks, for example, can learn to

Above *Chicks follow and learn from the mother hen and from each other about both food and safety.*

identify the potential traits of successful females by observing the appearance and behavior of their mothers, but female chicks can only learn about the appearance and behavior of successful males by observing other members of the flock.

For example, in many species of birds, including quail and other galliforms (see page 57), females pay close attention to which males are approached by other females ready to mate, and when they are approached. By learning about the mating preferences of other females, including older and more experienced hens, young chicks can avoid exposing themselves to roosters of poor quality later in life. They can also make sure that they only submit to the dangers of the mating process itself for a good-quality rooster.

Such "mate copying" is a socially successful strategy. Young hens "eavesdrop" on the courting behavior of males in order to observe the mate choices of other females. It is through this form of covert observation that they select their own mate in the future, which also explains why hens in different flocks can exhibit such differences in mate choice.

Chickens Behaving Badly

Anyone who has closely observed the behaviors of colonial seabirds, such as penguins or gannets, will know that nature has very little to do with peace, harmony, and equilibrium; neighboring birds frequently strike and hiss at each other, peck and draw blood, or severely damage and even kill others. Similarly, the behavior of captive birds housed at high densities will probably incorporate natural types of aggression and unnatural extensions of such behavior provoked by the conditions.

AGGRESSION BY FEMALES

Hens in a flock establish near-linear dominance hierarchies, with the outcome that the many pecks and blows delivered by a dominant individual to subordinate ones become commonplace. Yet, in high-density environments and with few places to hide, escape from such aggression is nearly impossible. The pecks become all the more common, causing feather loss and wounding, and inviting infections, which further weaken the subordinates' health and condition.

Even in backyards and other more open captive environments, aggression based on flock hierarchy can result in extensive damage or fatalities. This is especially true when new, unfamiliar individuals are introduced to the well-established flock. Such newcomers can suffer vicious mob attacks from the rest of the flock, eliminating any opportunity for one-on-one confrontations with individual flock members. Deprived of the chance to claim a role further up the hierarchy, newcomers inevitably end up at the bottom of the pecking order.

Females can also group together to attack a subordinate rooster in the pen or the yard; hens have clear preferences for the dominant male and try to avoid uninvited mating attempts by subordinates. When males become subordinate to the resident rooster in the flock, especially in a captive facility where the new males cannot escape, females might group together and attack the subordinate rooster. Such attacks can cause physical injury and even death, especially if the subordinate male is already weakened by attacks from the dominant rooster.

Below *Fighting is an everyday event in the daily routines of both roosters and hens.*

BAD NESTING HABITS

In many bird species, females avoid the cost of building a nest and taking care of their eggs by laying the eggs in others' nests and letting the foster parents look after the young. Through the process of domestication, it is more likely that such parasitic egg laying has been favored in chickens raised by captive breeding and artificial selection; females that laid their eggs in several nests would probably leave at least some progeny behind and, in turn, provide the next generation with more parasitic daughters.

Indeed, recent experiments with zebra finches have shown that simply removing the eggs of a laying female before her clutch is completed (whether due to predation in the wild or having the eggs collected for human needs) generates parasitically behaving females who prefer to lay the rest of their already ovulated and shelled eggs in the nests of other actively laying females. Some hens, in fact, strictly tend to lay in sites where other females' eggs have already been laid; accordingly, in captivity, a hen's nesting efforts can be prompted or redirected by placing fake eggs in a nest box—perhaps in a more accessible and easily manageable location for the keeper.

The consumption of high-protein diets, especially meats and eggs, can significantly increase the rates of types of aggression between hens.

All of these cases of "bad behavior" in hens can be alleviated by removing the object of attacks, including the injured female or male, or the freshly laid eggs, and, in general, by reducing the density of birds.

AGGRESSION BY MALES

Mating with a male typically transfers enough sperm to the female for her to fertilize her eggs for several weeks and months to come. Also, hens of many strains will readily lay unfertilized eggs and, unlike captive canaries and other songbirds, they do not require repeated exposure to the vocal or visual stimulus of a rooster calling and displaying to initiate and continue their egg-laying behaviors.

The presence of males is also a frequent source of aggression between the sexes. Subordinate males, for example, will attempt forced copulation with unwilling females. Even the dominant male, in a characteristic way, can appear aggressive and cause physical damage to a receptive female. This is because avian mating is an awkward process.

Like males in most birds species, but unlike ducks and paleognath birds (including ostriches, emus, rheas, kiwis, and tinamous), roosters do not have a large protruding organ to introduce to the female during copulation. Instead, they have to balance themselves by their feet on top of the female, often pulling on her head feathers with their beak to stay steady. They then turn their tail under the female's tail, aiming for a "cloacal kiss," during which the sperm is transferred.

The process can be as quick as a few seconds. Afterward, the female typically puffs up and shifts through her feathers, several of which will probably have been pulled out and others damaged. She will also have suffered peck and claw marks and other wounds. Such damage will be exacerbated if the female is involved in repeated copulations, which can occur if the density of the birds is too high and, especially, if the female-to-male ratio is too low in the yard or the cage.

The introduction of a new male into a pen or backyard "ruled" by an established rooster will cause an immediate rise in

Left *Mating in birds can result in mild-to-severe distress and even in missing feathers and open wounds caused to the female.*

Above *Physical fights between roosters are common and can result in major injuries or even death.*

the occurrence of aggressive behaviors. These include elevated crowing rates, physical attacks, and even fights to the death. Roosters have everything to lose by allowing a new competitor to establish himself within the flock, because hens base their choice of mate primarily on dominance, and only secondarily on courtship behaviors and sexual display traits. Therefore, maintaining dominance is critical to being a reproductively successful rooster, which is the sole currency of evolutionary fitness for both wild and captive animals.

SIGNS OF MALTREATMENT

- Keep an eye out for signs of chickens experiencing repeated mistreatment from other flock members, such as lost feathers and bloody patches of skin.
- Be ready to isolate the victims of bad behavior.
- Males are not needed for hens to lay eggs if breeding is not the goal.

CHAPTER 4

Intelligence & Learning

Intelligence & Learning ⟿

There are more chickens in the world than there are individuals of any other species of bird. Their ubiquitous presence in our daily lives, usually on our menus, often leads us to underestimate how their cognitive abilities have helped them to become such a successful domesticated species over the last 10,000 years.

To understand chicken intelligence, it is first necessary to understand that animal intelligence is not based on a single sliding scale, on which humans always represent the pinnacle of evolutionary success. Each species faces unique challenges in its environments. Some may need to dive under frigid water for four to five minutes at a time to catch fish; others may need to migrate thousands of miles to survive the winter.

Humans certainly do not have adaptations for all of these challenges; we cannot naturally use magnetic fields to navigate halfway around the globe, for example (although we have developed technologies that can). We consider ourselves highly intelligent because we have abilities to solve the environmental challenges that are relevant to our own survival.

In this sense, chickens are just as intelligent as humans, because their physical, behavioral, and cognitive abilities allow them to be successful at solving chicken-related challenges. An animal's intelligence must be judged in context; chickens are as smart as they need to be in order to be successful in the environments in which they have evolved.

FROM RESEARCH TO REALITY

Some of the cognitive abilities shown by chickens are only clearly evident when they are tested under controlled, experimental conditions. The fact that chicks prefer harmonic, pleasant-sounding music (consonant music) to unpleasant (dissonant) music is not something that is evident from watching them in a yard or on a farm. However, this recently discovered phenomenon might be linked to their innate preference to copy the behavior of (or imprint on) living objects instead of something inanimate. Animals generally produce more harmonic sounds, whereas inanimate objects do not.

Chicks also show the ability to add and subtract, and differentiate between groups with more objects or birds and those with fewer. These mathematical skills, easily overlooked when watching chickens busily foraging in their environments, may be important to their survival. Larger groups of birds may provide more protection from predators than smaller groups, so staying with the larger crowd may be the safer option. It is also more efficient to ignore smaller patches of food and seek out larger ones.

As more is discovered about chicken intelligence in laboratory settings, it becomes much easier to show how their cognitive abilities influence the types of behavior that we observe them perform on a day-to-day basis. We may never have the perfect answer to why the chicken crossed the road, but research continues to provide us with amazing insights into the mind of our most familiar feathered friend.

Below *Scientists continue to study what makes chickens tick— and what makes them cross the road.*

Inside the Brain

When we call something "bird-brained," we usually mean that it lacks intelligence, but research has shown this to be an inaccurate stereotype. There are many examples of complex cognitive abilities shown by bird species, including the domestic chicken.

Despite obvious differences in brain size and shape between birds and mammals, species from both groups have developed effective adaptations to cope with common challenges in their environments, such as finding food, interacting with members of the same species, and avoiding predators. The chicken brain certainly looks different from a generic mammalian brain, but these differences are purely cosmetic. In their own ways, chickens and their ancestors have been just as successful as humans at adapting to their environments.

The cortex, and especially neocortex, of the mammalian brain (the wrinkly outer part) was always thought to provide mammals with more advanced cognitive abilities, such as problem-solving skills and abstract thinking (for example, realizing that objects do not just disappear when they go out of sight). To understand why this is not actually accurate, it is necessary to explore some of the key similarities and differences seen in bird and mammal brains.

DIFFERENT EVOLUTIONARY PATH

One of the reasons that the chicken brain looks different from our own is that birds have been on a different evolutionary path from mammals for the last 300 million years—which is when birds and mammals' shared ancestor was thought to have lived. Over this time, birds have evolved cognitive abilities necessary for their survival, some of which far surpass those shown by mammals.

CEREBRUM

Functions include how we sense our environment, how we act upon this information, and what we are thinking about when we act.

CEREBELLUM

The large cerebellum in birds and mammals plays an important role in coordinating voluntary movement of muscle. In humans, this includes locomotion and the muscle movements involved in speech.

CEREBELLUM

In birds, the cerebellum is important for flight.

CEREBRUM

The cerebrum in birds serves much the same role as the mammalian cortex in processing sensory information and controlling behavior, although the structural design of the nerve tissues can be different.

HYPERPALLIUM

The arrangement of nerve cells in this part of the chicken brain is completely unique to birds.

HUMAN BRAIN

The most notable difference between the brain anatomy of chickens and the structure of mammal brains is the absence in the former of a well-defined cerebral cortex. This area of the brain in humans represents the conscious, thinking part of our central nervous system that gives us our unique abilities to think deep thoughts, experience a wide range of emotional states, and coexist successfully as part of an extremely social species.

CHICKEN BRAIN

Distantly related parts of the bird brain have taken on many of the functions performed by the mammalian cerebral cortex, meaning that different parts of the bird and mammal brain often control similar abilities. Since chickens face many of the same challenges as some of their group-living mammal counterparts, it is not surprising to find that they have come up with similar ways to overcome these challenges.

The chicken brain consists of two interconnected halves, or hemispheres. Each half controls the chicken's behavior and helps it process information about its environment in slightly different ways.

Human brains also have two hemispheres. The nerve cells controlling our vision and the muscles and limbs on the left-hand side of our bodies are generally found in the right (contralateral) hemisphere, and vice versa.

When different parts of the brain play different roles, this is known as lateralization. The degree of lateralization in the chicken brain is much more pronounced than in humans, especially when it comes to how they see the world around them.

Chickens can see the world in two different ways, either using both eyes together to look at an object (binocular vision) or using each eye to look at a completely separate image at the same time with no overlap of visual information between the eyes (monocular vision).

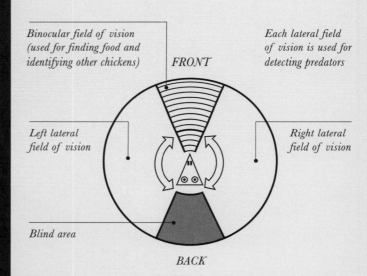

VISION

Binocular field of vision (used for finding food and identifying other chickens)

FRONT

Each lateral field of vision is used for detecting predators

Left lateral field of vision

Right lateral field of vision

Blind area

BACK

The field of binocular vision in chickens is approximately 26 degrees. Using their monocular vision (a combination of their left and right lateral fields), chickens have panoramic vision of about 300 degrees.

TAKING IN THE VIEW

Monocular vision, combined with the location of the eyes, gives a chicken the ability to see a panoramic view of its local environment. This is an advantage that chickens have in common with other prey species, such as cows, sheep, and horses, all of which need to keep an eye (or two) out for predators.

Because it is hard to judge distance when using only one eye, chickens rely on their binocular vision to help them forage for food items hidden within vegetation or on the ground. Binocular vision is also used to help chickens identify each other. Getting as much visual information as possible from both eyes at the same time helps chickens to recognize up to about 96 other individuals.

A BRAIN OF UNEQUAL HALVES

The lateralization of the chicken brain means that images seen by the right eye are processed in the left hemisphere of the brain, and those perceived by the left eye are processed by the right hemisphere. The way the chicken embryo is positioned in the egg during incubation also means that the two brain hemispheres develop differently (see pages 94–95).

Within the egg, the left side of the embryo's head is usually tucked under the wing as the chick nears maturity. This means that more natural light passes through the eggshell and reaches the right eye during a time when the nerve cells associated with vision are developing (days 19–21 of egg incubation).

This stimulates the growth of additional brain cells in the left hemisphere of the chicken's brain, and this asymmetry in brain development can affect the cognitive abilities and behavior of a chicken throughout its life.

A DIVISION OF LABOR

The right eye/left hemisphere in chickens is better at discriminating images into categories by identifying common features of objects. (Is this a piece of grain or a pebble? Is it a familiar chicken or not?)

The left eye/right hemisphere plays an important role in any learning involving spatial information, such as the location of an object in the chicken's environment. When a chicken hears recordings of other chickens making aerial alarm call vocalizations, which they give in response to the sight of a hawk flying overhead, it usually turns its head to view the sky with the left eye.

This sends the information to the right hemisphere of the brain, where fear responses are also controlled, ensuring that the chicken responds as quickly as possible to the danger.

DOUBLE EXPOSURE

Chickens can process two sets of visual information at the same time. They can keep one eye on the lookout for predators while looking for food items somewhere else with the other. This would be similar to a human driving a car with one eye looking forward and the other backward—something our eyes and brain are simply not equipped to do.

While we may wish for eyes in the back of our heads to give us this ability, chickens already excel at this with their laterally located eyes.

Left *Domestic chickens have been successful as farm animals because they are good at converting poor quality or hard-to-find food items into eggs and meat. Their visual system plays an important part in this success.*

THE RIGHT FOOD— THE LEFT HEMISPHERE

When foraging for food, chickens first look for areas in their environment that should contain something edible. They then identify appropriate, edible food items before the food (such as grain, insects) is eaten. Both hemispheres of the chicken brain work together to achieve this feat.

A potential food item, such as an insect, is first located in space using the left eye/right hemisphere system, and then the right eye/left hemisphere system allows the chicken to tell the insect apart from other similarly shaped or colored nonfood items in the local environment.

Ground-scratching behavior
When chickens search the ground for food, they perform a ground-scratching behavior with their feet. They scratch at the dirt first with one leg and then with a series of alternate scratches by both legs. It may be no coincidence that chickens usually start scratching with their right foot. This is the foot controlled by the left hemisphere of the brain. If the right foot uncovers a possible food item, it will be the right eye that sees this first.

Because the right eye/left hemisphere system is the one that chickens use to distinguish between food and nonfood items, the chicken will be able to tell immediately if it can eat it. Since the best food items can potentially get away if a chicken takes too long to make up its mind, the fact that the actions of the right leg, the right eye, and the left hemisphere are all coordinated makes chickens effective and efficient foragers.

INCUBATION CARE

- Remember that light makes a difference to the development of the chicken embryo within the egg—with a particular effect on its cognitive abilities.

- Make sure that incubated eggs are exposed to natural light, especially in the last few days before hatching. Chicks incubated this way will be better at discriminating between food and nonfood items and faster at spotting a potential predator within their environment. They also tend to form stronger and more stable social groups with other chickens, which can help to reduce levels of aggression.

- Eggs incubated in the dark can produce chickens that are more distressed when they see a potential predator in their environment, take longer to get back to their normal feeding behavior after this experience, and are more distracted by unimportant stimuli that appear in their environment.

Imprinting & Learning ~

When we picture imprinting in animals, such as chicks, ducklings, or goslings, we usually think of a newly hatched bird forming an instant bond with the first living thing they see.

A closer look reveals a complex learning process that involves a host of cognitive and sensory abilities shown by animals that are no more than a few hours old.

WHY IMPRINT?

Because chicks are mobile and can feed independently almost immediately after hatching, imprinting is crucial to their survival. They have all of the behavioral abilities of more adult birds, but none of the experience; they don't know what to eat, where to rest, or what types of animals or objects they should avoid.

With her greater experience, a hen can protect chicks from danger and help to shape their behaviors, preferences, and abilities through her actions. To learn from their hen, chicks must stay close to her so that they can watch what she does and where she does it. Imprinting is what makes the chicks stay so close by. Without it, they would be far less likely to survive or develop appropriate social and behavioral preferences later in life.

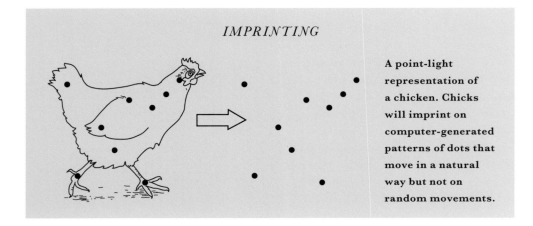

IMPRINTING

A point-light representation of a chicken. Chicks will imprint on computer-generated patterns of dots that move in a natural way but not on random movements.

Right *By imprinting
on their mother, chicks
remain close enough
to her to learn from
her example.*

FILIAL IMPRINTING

In the first 48 hours after hatching,
chicks focus their attention on and
become behaviorally attached to one
particular stimulus in their environment.
The technical term for this is "filial
imprinting." Under natural conditions
this stimulus will be the mother hen.

In her absence, chicks can imprint
on a range of nonchicken animals and
even nonliving objects. In fact, they have
natural preferences and sensory biases
for the types of stimuli that, when looked
at together, would most probably be a
mother hen—something that moves in
a biologically natural way and that has a
well-defined head and neck area with eyes.

MOVING OBJECTS

Many types of moving objects can be
successfully used as imprinting stimuli,
including other chickens, ducks, humans,
even potential predators, such as cats and
polecats, as well as nonliving objects that
are made to move in an artificial manner
(such as a movable stuffed chicken).

Some types of movement work
better than others—as demonstrated by
experiments using point-light animation.
This is a technique used by animation
studios to make the movement of their
animated characters more lifelike. It
involves placing reflective balls on all
the body joints, and then recording the
movement of the balls while the body is
in motion. The movement of only those
discrete points on the body, when played
back on a computer screen, is called a
point-light animation sequence.

Experiments show that chicks are just
as attracted to a point-light animation
sequence of a hen walking as they are to
a real hen walking. They are not attracted
to the dots themselves, or to the same dots
made to move in a random fashion. They
only respond when the dots move in a
biologically predictable manner.

Human babies do not imprint in the
same way as chicks, but they show a
similar preference for natural movement
and do not seem to mind whether it
comes from a human or an animal from
another species altogether. In chickens,
these sensory biases ensure that chicks do

not imprint upon rocks, plants blowing in the breeze, or other nonliving objects that cannot offer them care and protection.

THE "EYES" HAVE IT

Chicks show innate sensory preferences for heads and eyes, and these alone are enough for imprinting to occur. If chicks imprint on an artificial, nonliving object, they will usually shift their preference to a more naturalistic stimulus that includes a head and eye region, if they have a choice. Even as adults, only the head and neck areas of their companions need to be seen for recognition of individuals.

Under certain conditions, chicks that have imprinted on one stimulus can change their minds and imprint on a different one. They prefer natural objects with heads and eyes, but even a preference for a living hen can be reduced if they are separated from it for just a few hours. Imprinting is not irreversible, but something about the first living stimulus that chicks imprint on does seem to stick in their memory, and they will generally show a greater preference for it over other similar objects.

THE IMPRINTING CLOCK

The imprinting process is not instant. It can occur over a period of several hours after hatching. However, as they develop a preference for one type of object or animal, chicks become less receptive and less able to imprint on other stimuli. This makes it seem as if there is a sensitive window of time during which imprinting occurs. This window of time varies based on the chicks' exposure to appropriate

imprinting stimuli in their environment. So, the time it takes for chicks to imprint depends on the nature of their experiences observing different objects around them.

NO REWARD NEEDED

When dogs are trained to sit, they usually do so because they receive a positive reward, such as a treat from their owner. During the process of imprinting, chicks do not need to receive food, warmth, or even social companionship from the object in which they show an interest. Many of the artificial, nonliving stimuli that chicks can imprint on offer none of the maternal care that a hen provides, and yet can be just as attractive.

THE POWER OF SONG

After hatching, chicks can learn to recognize the distinctive calls of their hen, but they do not imprint on just these calls. They still need to see a visual stimulus. However, the sounds made by the hen can play a role in the imprinting process.

Many of the vocalizations made by hens in the vicinity of their chicks contain rhythmic, staccato elements (such as the "kuk-kuk-kuk" call given by the hen to attract chicks to a food item). These rhythmic calls have been found to speed up the imprinting process.

The sound cues make objects more attractive to the chicks and enhance the ability of chicks to learn and remember. Even artificial stimuli can be made more attractive to chicks if recordings of these rhythmic calls are played in their presence.

Right *Chicks will respond favorably to objects with the inverted triangular shape of a head, especially with well-defined eye areas.*

SEXUAL IMPRINTING

A second form of imprinting known as sexual imprinting occurs later in a chick's development over a number of days and weeks. Sexual imprinting ensures that, when chicks mature, their sexual behaviors are focused on appropriate individuals—members of the right species and sex (see page 106). The sexual preferences of mature birds seem to be based on the visual appearance and behaviors of not just the mother hen, but also other flock mates, too. This means that even birds that imprint on nonchicken objects can still show appropriate sexual behavior if reared with other chickens around them.

HELPING CHICKS IMPRINT

- If possible, let chicks imprint upon hens. This is the best way to make sure that they learn the social and behavioral preferences necessary for them to eat the right food, form stable relationships with other birds, and respond appropriately and nonaggressively to sexual partners as adults.

- If imprinting chicks on an artificial stimulus, provide a moving stimulus that has a defined head region with eyes. Use rhythmic calls as an additional encouragement.

- Keep in mind that chicks show a preference for red and blue objects over green or yellow ones during the process of imprinting.

Cognitive Ability

Many of the cognitive abilities shown by chickens are similar to those used by primates, and yet chickens are rarely thought of as being as intelligent as monkeys. Our closer genetic relationship with primates may bias our perspective, but a closer look at the way chickens think and act can open our eyes to the complex world of the cognitive chicken.

Intelligence and learning abilities are always related to the unique conditions a species faces in its natural environment. The cognitive abilities possessed by chickens are the same ones that proved to be so valuable for their jungle-fowl ancestors in the dense jungles of Southeast Asia. From this perspective, chickens are no more or less intelligent than any other species.

What is different about domestic chickens compared to their wild relatives is that the human-created environments they now find themselves in are different from the wild environments in which their cognitive abilities evolved. The domestic husbandry of chickens has led to comparatively new pressures on cognitive development, resulting in some new abilities in the realms of recognition, discrimination, and vocalization.

SOCIAL LIVING

The challenges of finding food and mates, successfully rearing young, and avoiding danger are common to all animals. Species living in highly social environments must deal with an additional layer of environmental complexity—the convoluted actions of members of their own groups (see pages 74–81).

Chickens form stable social groups made up of individuals with defined ranks forming a pecking order. This means that chickens can recognize who's who in their social group, but can also assign a rank to these different individuals.

Dominance is hard to quantify, especially as the biggest hens, or those with larger physical attributes (such as combs), are not always the most dominant individuals. When a hen responds differently to a dominant bird compared to a subordinate one, it has to remember its past experiences with those birds in terms of whether it won or lost out during any previous confrontations. It uses these direct experiences to guide its behavior. It can also use what it learns from watching other birds interact—making use of these indirect experiences as well.

KEEPING UP WITH
THE FARMER JONESES

Chickens can discriminate between different humans, recognizing those individuals they associate with positive experiences (such as food, social companionship) and those who have treated them poorly. This seems to occur most commonly when there is extensive contact between individual birds and their keepers.

Where contact between chickens and humans is minimal, chickens tend to generalize their experiences. An individual bird that has a few, limited experiences of positive contact with people will tend to show a reduced level of fear to people with whom they have never interacted before, regardless of any physical differences in their appearance or clothing.

If their interactions with humans are negative, then they may show generalized fear responses to all humans.

Left *A hen's cognitive abilities help it to remember its place within the complex social environment of a flock— whether that is at the top or bottom of the hierarchy.*

NOT JUST ALARM CLOCKS

Chickens do not use language to communicate in the same way that humans do, but they do have complex vocalizations (see pages 82–85). Chickens have around 24 unique vocalizations, each with slightly different meanings. Some provide information about the quality of food; others are contact calls that help birds to stay together even when they are physically out of sight from one another.

Chickens also give different types of alarm calls, with one given in response to the presence of aerial predators, and another made when ground-dwelling predators, such as foxes, raccoons, and snakes, are spotted.

When hens hear the loud sequence of pulses that make up the terrestrial predator alarm call, they usually respond by standing erect and scanning the horizon for movement. Typically, only male chickens produce the distinctive aerial predator alarm call. Stimuli that look like birds of prey are the most effective triggers, but insects, hot-air balloons, planes, and nonpredatory birds can also give rise to these calls. When hens hear this call, they crouch down, scan the sky, and attempt to seek shelter.

Knowing the audience
The ability to assign different calls to different predators, and to perform different behaviors in response to these different alarm calls, is usually attributed to only certain primate species. However, chickens are just as efficient at categorizing elements of their environment in this way. It has even been shown that males give more alarm calls when they are in the presence of hens, compared to when they are on their own or housed with animals from other species. They seem to show some sensitivity to who will be listening to what they have to say (see page 73).

Above *A chicken will crouch when an aerial predator alarm call is given, but will stand erect when warned of a terrestrial predator.*

Right *Domestic chickens rarely have difficulty finding food when reared commercially, and predators are less of an issue too. Their artificially supersocial environments often bring a range of new challenges though that can potentially affect their welfare.*

DEALING WITH DOMESTICATION

There is no clear evidence that the process of domestication reduces cognitive abilities in domesticated animals. While there is often a general reduction in overall brain size in domesticated species compared to their wild counterparts, information-processing skills and learning abilities seem unaffected.

Indeed, domesticated animals often are better at learning associations between cause and effect (such as between the behaviors they perform and the positive or negative consequences of those behaviors) in captive situations because they are less fearful of novel environments compared to wild animals. Fear can be a significant impediment to learning.

OUT OF SIGHT IS NOT NECESSARILY OUT OF MIND

In human infants, it takes about eight months before a baby shows an understanding that objects that disappear behind a visual barrier are still actually there. Chicks, however, can show this same ability within the first week of their lives; when the object they have imprinted on goes out of sight, chicks can continue to remember its location for at least three minutes.

Adult hens also show a similar ability to respond to stimuli that are not physically present. Hens with no previous experience of dust bathing and nesting areas show similar amounts of searching behaviors as birds with previous experience that have been deprived of them. They seem to be aware that some behavioral opportunity is absent from their environment.

The Effects of Domestication ⌇

Species living in the wild are often regarded as smarter than their domesticated relatives because they face an environment full of daily uncertainty without the care of humans to help them survive and thrive. As with many mammal species, the domestication process in birds has typically led to a 24–35 percent reduction in brain size in domesticated animals compared to their wild counterparts.

However, a decreased brain size does not mean that the domestic chicken is less intelligent than its ancestors. After all, the domestic dog has a smaller brain than a wolf, but its potential to sniff out drugs and explosives, and to detect when epileptics are about to have a seizure, or when diabetics are about to experience a low blood sugar episode, speaks to their astounding cognitive abilities.

SUPERSOCIAL

Over the course of their domestication, chickens have not become integrated into the human world in the same way that dogs have become "part of the family," but many of their cognitive abilities remain well suited to the new human-created environments in which they find themselves. These environments are usually more socially complex than those experienced by jungle fowl, because domesticated birds need to understand and respond to the actions of humans and other chickens. These environments are often supersocial, with hundreds or thousands of birds housed together in the same space.

Below Domestication does affect brain size, but there are few obvious behavioral differences between jungle fowl and their domestic counterparts.

familiar objects, rather than to a group containing only two objects, even remains when these groups are hidden behind two separate opaque screens.

Chicks can remember which screen hides the larger grouping, and can even do the math when they observe objects being taken out from behind one screen and moved to behind the other one. They still choose the screen hiding the largest group after changes have been made.

Because a brood of chicks contains about eight to ten fast-moving siblings with a tendency to move in and out of sight, having the cognitive ability to keep track of this number of objects in space is a great social advantage, and it may be beneficial even in environments where there are hundreds of birds.

TELLING THE TIME

Roosters may know what time the sun rises, but hens also seem to have a basic notion of time. Hens can learn to peck at a computer screen after a fixed period of time in order to receive a food reward, and can continue to respond accurately even after durations of about six minutes.

Because humans commonly apply arbitrary time constraints to their own activities (such as a one-hour lunch break), this skill may help chickens anticipate our actions more effectively when we share environments. For example, if hens can predict how long a quick veterinary checkup might last (such as when they are being physically restrained by a human in a way that they might not find pleasant), they may not take such an aversion to the situation.

A HEAD FOR NUMBERS

It can pay to have a good head for numbers when living in a complex social environment, and even chicks can use basic arithmetic skills to help them navigate their way around.

Chicks prefer to be with a larger group of familiar companions or objects than a smaller one. This is a good way to avoid becoming separated from the rest of their flock mates and the mother hen. Their preference to be close to a group of three

Social Learning

Living in groups provides chickens with opportunities to benefit from the behavior of their flock mates. Extra pairs of eyes, for example, can help scan the environment more effectively for predators, and successful foraging by one bird can help others learn how or where to find food.

As a poorly flighted, ground-dwelling (and tasty) prey species, the ancestors of the domestic chicken survived thanks directly to the benefits gained from group living. Domestic chickens today still have the cognitive abilities to make the most of their social environment in which other chickens can serve as caregivers, competitors, aggressors, demonstrators, and even teachers.

Within a social group, chickens learn about the world around them using their own individual experiences, and by observing the behavior and experiences of other group members. This second process is called social learning.

Left *Chicks learn from each other as well as adult birds.*

SOCIAL LEARNING
IN CHICKS

When newly hatched chicks begin to forage, they rely on social learning to help them identify appropriate food items to feed on. They do not automatically know what is edible and inedible; they peck at any objects that are about ⅛ inch (3–4 mm) in diameter, and do not seem to learn from their own experiences how to be more discerning. Instead, their attention must be drawn toward appropriate food by the vocalizations and pecking behavior of the mother hen.

These feeding displays are made with more intensity when the hen is near good-quality food, and when chicks appear to be feeding from inappropriate food or nonfood items. The behavior of hens, then, helps to redirect the chicks' behavior to more appropriate foods, in what could be described as a form of directed teaching. Day-old chicks can also respond to the feeding behavior of other chicks, and they will avoid pecking at a bitter food after watching other chicks tasting it and reacting in disgust.

The development of the chick brain continues after it hatches. At around 10–11 days, chicks begin to move farther away from the stimulus they have imprinted upon and start to explore their surroundings more widely. In a complex environment, this often means that chicks will move out of direct sight from the mother hen and other chicks, even if just for a short time.

Spatial memory
The experience of objects disappearing from sight and then reappearing in a predictable manner is essential for the development of effective spatial memory and social learning abilities.

These cognitive abilities allow chicks to remember the number and type of objects that become hidden or obscured, as well as what behaviors they saw other animals perform and in what location. Imitation of behavior is one way animals can learn from other animals. Remembering where an animal performed a feeding behavior, for example, is one way that a bird can increase its own chances of being a successful forager.

Food is usually found in clumps (such as a head of wheat, a bowl of food, a collection of insects and worms under a stone), so the combination of a good spatial memory and an ability to imitate behaviors is helpful.

SOCIAL LEARNING
IN ADULTS

Adult birds continue to show an ability to learn from the feeding behavior of their flock mates, but after about nine weeks of age they begin to rely on their own personal experiences to a greater degree.

Given a choice between two foods of different colors, adult birds that watch other hens eating only one color of the food show a preference for food of that same color. However, they become less likely to avoid pecking at food that triggers disgust responses in other birds.

This change in the influence of social learning occurs at about the time that the

birds become more independent, and the individual experiences of these maturing birds become much more important.

It may be more advantageous for individual birds to make their own minds up about what is and is not good food, for example, so that they do not lose out on potential food sources that other birds have yet to uncover.

At this age, chickens also become more selective when it comes to responding to social cues. Chicks, for example, will head for a food source if it is pointed out by an arrow moving up and down nearby; adults will not.

Dominant birds

Hens also seem to learn more from watching dominant birds than they do from watching subordinate or unfamiliar ones, and they seem to learn little from watching roosters.

The fact that dominant hens make the best demonstrators is not due to the fact that they are the biggest animals (roosters are bigger), or that they are the best foragers or decision makers. It is because dominant birds are most likely to exert their dominance in an aggressive manner, causing subordinate birds to observe them much more closely—if only to make sure that they can stay out of their way and avoid being pecked.

The more closely subordinate birds watch dominant hens, the more probable it is that they will see what they are doing, and where, and be able to imitate the behavior in a similar setting.

Right *Subordinate hens observe dominant birds closely to learn from their behavior, and to avoid confrontation.*

REARING CHICKS

- Provide a structurally complex rearing environment—with different levels, food items, and objects to climb on, hide behind, and sit under. This encourages chickens to develop their social learning abilities fully.

- If possible, allow chicks to be reared by a hen. This will ensure that they develop appropriate feeding and dust-bathing preferences for the rest of their lives.

- Give chickens enough space in which to watch other birds without having to physically interact. This promotes observational learning. Subordinate birds learn more effectively if they are not being pecked at by more dominant individuals in the flock.

Living in a Hierarchy

The social structure of the domestic chicken closely mirrors that of its jungle-fowl relatives and ancestors. Where hens and roosters live together, small groups of hens form cohesive groups under the watchful gaze of a dominant rooster. Subordinate males hang around the periphery to avoid close encounters with the more aggressive alpha male.

Hens tend to be aggressive to unfamiliar hens, but physical aggression between familiar birds is usually low once they have established their position in the pecking order. A stable hierarchy allows dominant birds to use behavioral threat displays instead of physical aggression whenever there is competition for resources, such as food or perching spots.

As long as subordinate birds respond to these displays appropriately, usually by getting out of the way, then physical aggression can be avoided.

THE KEY TO A HIERARCHY

Stable social hierarchies only work when birds can recognize who is familiar and who is unfamiliar, and more importantly, who is dominant. Domestic chickens are housed in many different types of social situations, from small groups of five to six birds, to thousands of birds housed in the same space. In smaller groups, hens usually have linear pecking orders. This means that the most dominant hen gets what she wants regardless of which other hen she interacts with.

At the bottom of the pecking order, the subordinate bird has to keep an eye on all the other hens in the group, because any one of them could act aggressively toward her if she is not submissive enough.

Hens in the middle of the hierarchy have to change the way they behave, depending on which other hen they are interacting with. Remembering who's who in the pecking order is an important part of a chicken's cognitive abilities.

FRIEND OR FOE

Newly hatched chicks can tell familiar and unfamiliar animals apart after only 12 hours of direct contact with other chicks. Physical contact makes this ability to discriminate even more effective than just visual contact.

Given a choice, chicks prefer to be with familiar birds. They tend to peck more at unfamiliar chicks of the same age. Pecking can be an aggressive act, but it can also be a way to socialize; it gets birds in close proximity, enabling both to get a better look at each other.

Close contact and the use of binocular vision are needed for one hen to be able to recognize another individual. Visually, the best range is 3–12 inches (8–30 cm). Sound and smell can also help, but if hens cannot see each other, these other stimuli are not enough to allow for recognition.

The left eye/right hemisphere of the chicken brain plays the greatest role in recognition and discrimination of individual birds. From the eleventh day posthatch, chicks begin to favor their left eye when observing other birds.

This division of labor in the brain is seen in many other species; it is the right hemisphere of the human brain that is most involved in recognizing people and responding to their facial expressions.

Right *Chickens use their binocular vision to help them recognize familiar and unfamiliar birds, or dominant and subordinate ones. Aggressive pecks are usually directed towards the head and comb of other birds.*

PECKING ORDERS

Hens start jostling for rank only a week or so after hatching, and by six weeks pecking orders are already established. The process begins when hens act aggressively to other familiar birds when competing for resources, such as food. Hens that win aggressive interactions establish dominance over the losers.

Some of the factors that influence a hen's position in a pecking order include its hormone levels (for example, higher levels of testosterone are linked to higher levels of aggressiveness), body size, comb size, shape, and color, and previous experience of either winning or losing aggressive encounters (see pages 74–76).

The number of hens in a group determines which of these factors is most important. A hen can potentially recognize and remember up to ninety six individual hens.

In larger groups where birds continuously interact with unfamiliar animals, hens tend to assess dominance by referring to generalized physical characteristics, such as size of body or redness of comb. In smaller groups, they can recognize an individual's place in a pecking order using subtler methods.

This means that in large groups it is more common to see fights over resources; nonaggressive threat displays are not as effective when hens do not automatically know their place in the pecking order.

THE SPECTATOR EFFECT

Chickens use a basic form of logical reasoning to understand where they fit into social hierarchies. Instead of basing their assessment only on the number of actual aggressive interactions they win or lose with other birds, they also observe interactions between other birds.

If bird A is a dominant known to the observer, but unknown bird B beats bird A, then the observer is likely to see B as dominant. This means that the observer does not have to challenge every unknown bird or flock mate to a potentially dangerous aggressive encounter to determine rank.

Hens are more effective at using these logical deductions than roosters. This is not surprising given the social complexities faced by hierarchical hens.

THE HUMAN FACTOR

Chickens can recognize individual humans just as we can recognize our favorite chickens. The left eye/right hemisphere visual system is responsible for recognizing the configurations of a characteristic face, discriminating between different faces, and controlling the behaviors performed in response to these faces.

Chicks that have never seen a human before respond with fear to the gaze of a human face or lifelike mask. They focus most of their attention on our eyes, and show greater fear responses when they are stared at directly.

Eyes are an important stimulus to prey species, such as chickens, especially because many bird and mammal predators have clearly defined, large, and often forward-facing eyes. A model of a hawk can induce fear responses in chicks, but the chicks are less fearful if the eyes of the model are covered up.

Left *Hens watch interactions between other birds to work out their position in the hierarchy.*

SOCIAL RULES

- Avoid introducing unfamiliar birds to a small social group. Familiar hens can sometimes group together and attack newcomers, who can find it hard to establish a place in the pecking order (see page 108). High levels of aggression can lead to increased feather pecking, serious injuries, and even cannibalism.

- Maintain a positive relationship with your chickens. Chickens can individually recognize their keepers, and will remember positive and negative experiences they have had with them. The presence of people with whom chickens associate negative experiences can trigger fear responses and lead to other forms of negative emotional states, such as anxiety.

- Make sure that incubated eggs are exposed to periods of natural light. Chickens reared this way form more stable social hierarchies; they are better able to spot subtle social interactions between different ranked birds and figure out who is who in the hierarchy.

Food & Learning ~

Even a casual observer of chickens will notice that they tend to perform the same types of behaviors at the same time, and often in the same location, as their companions. This is called behavioral synchrony and it may help chickens stay together as a cohesive group—something that would have helped their jungle-fowl ancestors to survive. The tighter the group, the more likely it is that one member will spot an approaching predator and alert the others.

Behavioral synchrony depends on hens being able to respond to each other's actions. Hens, for example, eat more—and eat more vigorously—in the company of other hens than when alone. In fact, whether they have just eaten or are already hungry, hens become more motivated to eat when they see other birds feeding.

This is common in social species, and is one reason why restaurants like to seat customers in their window seats so that passersby can see people dining.

ENVIRONMENTAL CUES

Chickens can respond to different social cues to synchronize their behavior, but there are also obvious environmental factors at play. The delivery of food at the same time each day, for example, will usually result in synchronous feeding, and the approach of night-time will prompt birds to find a suitable perch for the night.

AN EYE FOR DETAIL

Sometimes the feeding behavior of a bird draws the attention of other birds to what it is eating. Feeding synchrony can then occur when the observers try to eat the food as well.

By paying attention to what behaviors other birds are performing and where, observers can learn about additional resources that they can also exploit (such as a new-found stash of grubs or grain, or a good spot for dust bathing).

PULLING RANK

A dominant hen that sees another bird feeding usually has no trouble muscling her way in to gain access to the food herself. A subordinate bird may not be able to do the same to a dominant bird—at least not without risking an aggressive encounter.

If subordinate hens observe a bird performing a behavior in a particular location, they may not immediately move to that location or copy the behavior. Instead they commit the location or behavior to memory and come back at a later time to exploit the resource.

COPYING THE GOOD, THE BAD, & THE UNWANTED

Unwanted behaviors can also be copied and imitated. If large flocks of chickens are housed in poor-quality environments, unwanted behaviors, such as aggression, feather pecking, and cannibalism, can arise.

Some of these can initially result from misdirected foraging and dust-bathing behaviors—common in birds reared without a hen to guide them. After that, it may be the behavior itself that attracts attention, or it may be broken feathers or a red bloody area on the birds affected by these abnormal behaviors (see pages 108–111).

HOUSING

- House birds in small groups; they are less likely to indulge in unwanted behaviors than those reared in flocks of hundreds or thousands.

- If birds must be housed in large groups, arrange resources, such as dust-bathing areas, perches, food, and water, so that as many birds as possible can perform the same behavior at the same time. Otherwise frustration can trigger outbreaks of aggression.

- Alternatively, break up the housing with opaque partitions. This reduces the social stimulus to perform the same behavior at the same time, minimizing competition for resources and observational learning of unwanted behaviors.

Training

Every interaction between humans and domestic chickens is an opportunity for training, just as it is with a cat or dog. Whether the keeper is aware of it or not, training can be taking place, often with unwanted consequences. If, for example, a cat has an irritating habit of scratching at the bedroom curtains at night, its owner might try to stop it by getting up and offering it a bowl of food downstairs. What this teaches the cat, however, is that scratching at the curtains gets it food—and it will carry on scratching all the more.

Domestic chickens share a similar capacity to learn about the consequences of their own behavior—understanding the principle of cause and effect—and even learn from the experiences of other chickens. Their inquisitive nature makes them easy to train, whether responding to commands to perform a natural behavior (like wing flapping), or performing some human-derived task (pecking at a specific area on a touch-screen computer).

Right *The inquisitive nature of chickens often makes them easy to train, and they can be very motivated to work for rewards.*

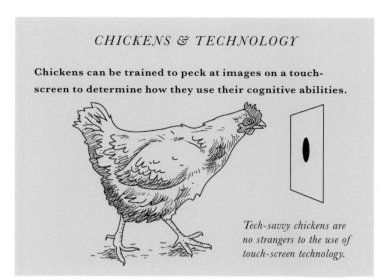

CHICKENS & TECHNOLOGY

Chickens can be trained to peck at images on a touch-screen to determine how they use their cognitive abilities.

Tech-savvy chickens are no strangers to the use of touch-screen technology.

CAUSE & EFFECT

It is easy for a chicken to make an association between the sound of food being prepared, or the sight of a bag containing food, with the food itself. Chickens can also anticipate the arrival of food based on human behavior (what we are doing and where we are doing it). They respond to these stimuli as if they are responding to the food itself.

These responses illustrate a basic form of learning common in all mammals and birds called classical conditioning. If the sight of a bag of food predicts the arrival of food, then chickens will gather around and show an increase in foraging-type behaviors, such as scratching at the ground. If the sight of a transport cage accurately predicts that birds are going to be captured and restrained for a medical procedure, then chickens that have made this association may show fear and stress responses before any rounding up begins.

REWARDING BEHAVIORS

Training chickens by rewarding behaviors we want to see more of, like giving a treat to a dog when it sits, is a form of "operant conditioning." Chickens are quickly able to make the connection between the behavior they perform and the consequences associated with it, such as being rewarded with food, or being punished with something unpleasant, such as a loud noise, puff of air, or aggressive interaction. All animals will usually perform a rewarded behavior more frequently, but only when the reward immediately follows the behavior.

CONTROL

Hens will readily learn to press a button, or perform similar artificial tasks, when they are rewarded with food. During this type of training, it is the actions of the bird that controls whether a reward is received, so long as they understand what the trainer is asking of them.

Control is obviously important to chickens because they will continue to work for food (such as peck at a button) in situations where they also have access to freely available food—a phenomenon known as "contrafreeloading." Domestic chickens seem to place greater value on the rewards they receive when they have actively spent time and energy earning them.

Having some element of control can even make up for other environmental deficiencies. The stress responses shown by birds housed in inadequate environments, for example, are reduced when birds are provided with control—meaning that the behaviors they perform have predictable and positive outcomes.

CHICKEN GAMES

Chickens have the cognitive ability to remember an impressive sequence of behavioral tasks. By being trained in each task separately, and then having them combined, a hen can peck at a button to gain access to a perch hanging over a tank of water, cross the perch, pull on a string three times to open a door, choose the right arm at the end of a T maze, and then jump across water to gain

access to a nest box. While a chicken at the start of this sequence may not necessarily have the goal of the nest box in its mind, it can still successfully complete this chain of trained behaviors.

Humans exploit some of these learning abilities when chickens are used as live contestants in games of tic-tac-toe against paying humans. Chickens peck at a screen as if they are making a move in response to the human's move. In reality, the choice made by the human turns on a light above the screen for the chicken. This serves as the cue for the bird to peck at the screen to get food (pecking at the screen when the light is off never makes food arrive).

Once the food arrives, a computer makes the actual choice of move on the chicken's behalf, but it still appears to the casual observer as if the chicken is playing the game.

INSTINCTIVE DRIFT

Foraging behavior, particularly scratching the ground for food, is deeply engrained in chickens. It is possible, for example, to train a chicken to stand still for a short period of time—a deeply unnatural behavior that is highly unlikely to result in successful foraging.

However, chickens trained this way often begin to show increasing amounts of scratching behavior, even if it is not rewarded. Even when chickens feed from food troughs or bowls, they still tend to perform scratching behaviors in or around the food. This highlights the evolutionary importance of these types of foraging behaviors in helping chickens to find food.

Right *Chickens display great behavioral flexibility, and can be trained to perform a wide range of artificial behaviors for access to food rewards, but they will still perform scratching behavior.*

Understanding Chicken Preferences

Domestic chickens have about 24 unique vocalizations that can reveal a lot about how they experience the world. For example, the gakel call (a whining long note followed by a series of short punctuated notes) is often given by chickens frustrated in their attempts to perform certain behaviors or gain access to resources.

Despite the complexities of chicken vocalizations, the one thing that they cannot do is reveal what they most like or dislike about their environments. For that, scientists have to use other methods.

SHORT-TERM PREFERENCE TESTS

In experiments, chickens can be placed in a run that forks in a Y or T shape, with an option visible in either direction. In these tests, chickens literally vote with their feet by moving toward their chosen option. Using this approach, hens have shown that they prefer to approach a familiar hen rather than an unfamiliar one, and prefer a small space with litter for foraging and dust bathing over a much larger barren space with only a wire floor. However, such tests can only reveal short-term preferences. Factors, such as the time of day, weather, presence of companions, and hunger can all affect what an individual bird might prefer from one moment to the next. Also, a preference for one type of resource does not necessarily mean that another is no good. Other forms of testing are required.

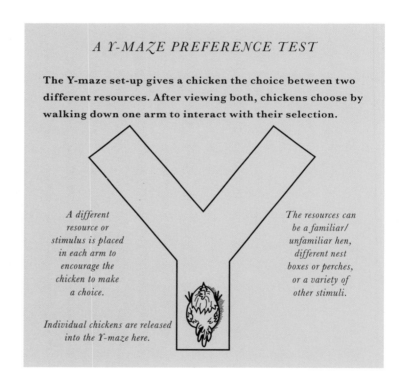

A Y-MAZE PREFERENCE TEST

The Y-maze set-up gives a chicken the choice between two different resources. After viewing both, chickens choose by walking down one arm to interact with their selection.

A different resource or stimulus is placed in each arm to encourage the chicken to make a choice.

The resources can be a familiar/ unfamiliar hen, different nest boxes or perches, or a variety of other stimuli.

Individual chickens are released into the Y-maze here.

LONGER-TERM PREFERENCE ASSESSMENTS

Longer-term preference tests can reveal a greater depth of information. Given the ability to turn lights off and on, chickens show a preference for at least four hours of light per day.

The amount of time that chickens spend in areas of their environment can also be interpreted as a choice. Free-roaming chickens prefer outside areas with trees and vegetation that provide overhead cover, compared to wide, open spaces. Birds spend more time outside and more time beneath the trees if given this choice.

Like jungle fowl, chickens tend to avoid large, open areas because these expose them to attack from a bird of prey or ground predator. Chickens prefer a habitat where there are open spaces they can view from the safety of denser vegetation. This gives them the ability to see potential predators coming and to disappear into the undergrowth if they do.

CHANGES OF MIND

In humans, past experiences can affect future preferences. If you grow up eating licorice, later in life the chances are you will like licorice more than a contemporary trying it for the first time.

Chickens can also get set in their ways. When faced with a choice between an enclosed cage and the outdoors, hens reared in the cage environment initially prefer this choice because they choose what they know. Once hens gain experience with the outdoors, their preference shifts to this more suitable habitat. So, initial preference is not the same as absolute preference, and chickens can change their minds.

STRENGTH OF PREFERENCES

We can get a much better idea of chickens' preferences if we monitor the amount of effort they are prepared to make for a particular thing. We know, for example, that hens like to perch off the ground at night because this is a better way to avoid predators. Moreover, we know that this is a strong preference because experiments have shown that hens are willing to push through an increasingly weighted door to access such perches.

We know also that hens like to have access to an enclosed nest box. The strength of this preference is shown by the fact that the closer the hens come to the time of egg laying, the more effort they are willing to make to squeeze through narrow gaps or push through doors to reach a suitable box. In fact, the effort made by hens to access nest boxes has been shown to match the effort they expend in reaching food after an enforced break of eight hours.

Similar experiments and observations have shown that chickens will work harder to gain access to some individuals rather than others. Roosters will work for access to unfamiliar roosters, because their desire to exert their dominance in

Above As egg-laying time approaches, hens become increasingly motivated to gain access to a nest box or dark secluded space.

an aggressive manner is strong. Hens, on the other hand, do not work hard for access to roosters at all; in many cases out of sight is out of mind when it comes to interaction with males. The amount of work that a hen will put in to access another hen depends on familiarity and rank, with hens less likely to work hard for access to unfamiliar or dominant birds.

Other types of experiment have been used to put a value on other known preferences. We know that chickens like a spacious environment, but how much space is enough? To test this, groups of chickens have been trained to peck at buttons that either increase or decrease the size of their enclosure. It seems that different birds often have conflicting preferences. Dominant birds may prefer smaller spaces, because they can more easily gain access to resources and keep other birds away from them. Subordinate birds may prefer larger spaces to avoid interactions with more dominant birds.

Below The strong preference that chickens show for roosting up high is inherited from their jungle fowl ancestors, who relied on tree roosts to protect themselves from hungry nocturnal predators.

GIVING CHICKENS CHOICE

- If chickens have access to the outdoors, make sure areas of open ground are broken up with objects, such as trees or bushes. Such objects can provide shade, shelter, food, and protection from birds of prey.

- Make sure there are a sufficient number of nesting areas for the majority of birds to use at the same time. Hens about to lay eggs are highly motivated to find a dark secluded spot to do so, and will fight for it, if necessary.

- Make sure there is enough perching space. Given the opportunity, all birds will perch at night, especially when there is enough space for subordinate hens to avoid close, aggressive encounters with more dominant birds.

Emotion & Welfare ~~~

Below *The emotional state of a hen when she lays her eggs affects how her chicks will respond to different situations.*

It is difficult to understand how chickens experience emotions when we do not even know for sure whether other humans feel emotional experiences in exactly the same way as we do. Many species of bird and mammal have the neurological machinery to generate emotional and behavioral responses that look like fear, frustration, pain, and even pleasure.

We may never know for sure whether they actually consciously experience these emotional states with the same clarity that we do. It is also possible that chickens have unique emotional states that we do not and cannot experience as humans.

THE BENEFIT OF EMOTIONS

Emotional states are beneficial because they tend to keep animals away from potentially harmful situations (such as predators, aggressive companions, noxious food items) and encourage animals to obtain resources that maximize survival (for example, food, warmth, shelter, companionship). The more important something is to survival, such as food, the more likely it is that a chicken will experience a positive emotional state when they are able to obtain it.

*Greater challenges with filial imprinting
on appropriate stimuli*

*Greater fear responses to
novel stimuli as adult birds:*

*Generally more sensitive
to environmental changes:*

• *New birds and new people*

• *Social environment*

• *New locations, foods, and
objects in their environment*

• *Physical/human
environment*

Early fear responses

Overt fear responses to new stimuli are noticed in chicks during the first few days after they have hatched and soon after they have imprinted on the mother hen or other stimulus. Experiencing fear at this age keeps chicks close to familiar objects, such as the hen and brood mates, which is essential for their survival, when they cannot yet regulate their temperature or avoid predators effectively.

INHERITING EMOTIONS

The emotional state of a mother hen around the time that she lays fertilized eggs can influence the future cognitive abilities of her chicks. When chickens respond to a stressful environment, they show an increase in the levels of stress hormones in their body known as corticosterones. These hormones help to prime the body of the chicken for useful action in response to stress—our normal "fight or flight" responses.

If the hen's environment is stressful just as she is about to lay her fertilized eggs, then high levels of these hormones will be deposited in the eggs. At high levels, corticosterones can interfere with normal cognitive development during egg incubation.

This "prenatal stress" effect can reduce the chicks' preferences to imprint correctly upon stimuli resembling a head and a neck during filial imprinting. Chicks that hatch from eggs containing high levels of corticosterones are also generally more fearful throughout their lives and more sensitive to changes in their environment.

We may not know whether chickens have the capacity to love, grieve, or experience joy or suffering, but it is a different thing altogether to know that what happens to an individual bird matters to that bird. Cockfighting, for example, is not a competition between two mindless entities, and birds in cramped, dark, and dirty cages are not just going about their business as if they were out in more natural conditions. If chickens cannot perform behaviors that they want to, or avoid situations that they want to get away from, the potential for suffering exists—even if that suffering is different from suffering as we ourselves understand it.

NEGATIVE EMOTIONAL STATES

Chicks separated from their social companions show a high frequency of distress vocalizations that suggest an anxiety-like state. The frequency of these vocalizations decreases with prolonged separation, which may indicate a more depression-like state. Negative experiences, such as social isolation, do seem to matter to chickens and can influence their behavior and long-term health, as well as the decisions they make.

Chickens housed in poor-quality environments make behavioral choices that appear to be pessimistic compared to chickens housed in more appropriate conditions. They might assume that the rustling noise in the undergrowth will more probably be something bad, such as a predator, instead of thinking it could be just another chicken foraging for food. This type of cognitive bias can be used as one way of identifying poor welfare, because pessimistic animals are more likely to experience fear or anxiety in their environments.

When chickens are prevented from participating in behaviors they want to perform, such as feeding, dust bathing, perching, or using a nest box, they show

Below *Aggression between chickens can have a significant impact on the welfare of the beaten bird.*

Above *Chickens can easily become frustrated if they are denied the opportunity to exhibit their natural behaviors.*

evidence of frustration. Just like humans, frustrated chickens often become more aggressive. They even give a particular type of vocalization known as a gakel call (see page 146) that can be used as another way to see if an environment is meeting their behavioral needs. More of these calls could mean that birds are being frustrated by a lack of suitable behavioral opportunities.

Trying to prevent long-term negative emotional states in chickens is important because individual birds can be affected by the emotional states experienced by other chickens. Domestic chickens show evidence of empathy when responding to the negative experiences of other birds. Hens that observe their chicks receiving a mildly unpleasant stimulus, such as a puff of air, show increases in heart rate and alertness, direct more vocalizations at the chicks, and preen less—all responses that have been associated with fear in hens.

This could mean that hens have the capacity not only to identify what other birds are feeling, but also to share these emotional states.

HAPPY CHICKENS

- Make sure that chickens do not associate you or any of their other keepers with negative emotional states. Birds exhibiting fear may injure themselves or other birds and will expend energy trying to escape the perceived threat. Chickens showing fear responses to humans tend to lay fewer eggs, show reduced growth, and convert the food they eat into meat or eggs less efficiently than nonfearful birds. Chronic fear by itself can result in health issues and potential suffering, even in the absence of physical injuries.

- Remember that chickens can recognize negative emotional states in other chickens and can be similarly affected by them. Creating management systems that minimize fear and frustration will improve the welfare of the flock as a whole.

- Create a stress-free environment for hens laying fertile eggs; this will ensure that the chicks do not show any cognitive disadvantages.

CHAPTER 5

Breeds

Fancy Fowl & the Chicken Frenzy of the Nineteenth Century ❧

Chickens have been kept by humans for thousands of years, but it is only in the past couple of centuries that any serious attention has been paid to chicken breeds and breeding. This interest was first kindled in the early nineteenth century, when trade channels started to open between China and the West. Suddenly, huge, exotic birds, such as the Cochin and Brahma, began to appear in the markets of Europe and North America, and ownership of them quickly became a symbol of wealth and taste.

In Great Britain, Queen Victoria herself became caught up by this new trend, which of course stimulated even more interest in the fashionable circles around her. By the mid-nineteenth century, in the space of just a few decades, chickens had gone from being simple backyard "eggers" to being sought-after prize poultry. A so-called "Hen Fever" had taken grip and landowners devoted space, time, and money to the prestige of evolving new breeds and colors.

Keepers throughout the Western world started to appreciate the incredible diversity of breeds that had wandered virtually unnoticed by earlier generations. They also began to understand more and more about how to "create" and "modify" the look of a bird by selective breeding.

As with the longer-standing interest in cattle and sheep breeding, the next inevitable step was to exhibit these birds at shows. The trend started out at smaller local events, where breeds, such as Sebrights and Pheasant Fowl, began to be seen in competition, but things soon snowballed. In 1845, Great Britain held its first sizable poultry show at London's Regent's Park Zoo. Then, in 1949, the United States followed suit when 10,000 people turned out to view almost 1,500 birds penned at Boston Public Gardens.

The enthusiasm shown by the exhibitors and visitors was such that over the second half of the nineteenth century large, carefully organized regional shows began to emerge, with some countries successfully hosting "Nationals." Competition was fierce and there was debate over the criteria by which the

chickens were judged. In 1865, to ensure consistency among the judges, the first record of poultry standards—the British Poultry Standard—was published by the then Poultry Club of Great Britain. The American Poultry Association followed suit in 1874 with its Standard of Perfection.

Initially, these standards covered only a handful of breeds, but numbers increased as more breeds were imported and developed. By the turn of the twentieth century, the number of classes within a show could easily exceed 100. In pursuit of ever-increasing prize money and prestige, exhibitors would send their "show team" of poultry on the show circuit for months on end. Today, the level of prize money has dropped to the extent that exhibiting poultry can only be a hobby, not a career. However, the competition to exhibit the "best in show" bird remains as strong as it ever was. The preservation of most chicken breeds, therefore, is assured.

Dual-Purpose Breeds

HISTORY

Dual-purpose, or utility breeds, hark back to the time before industrial agriculture and large-scale poultry farming. They were developed during the early part of the twentieth century as a composite of layer and meat breed types.

The intention was to create an accessible form of livestock for the small-scale farmer—one capable of providing both eggs and meat without being heavily biased toward either function.

This "functionality" would also make them ideal for breeding replacement stock, avoiding the need to run different pens of birds for eggs and for meat. The hens would be used primarily for egg production, whereas the surplus of males could be fattened to provide a cheap source of meat protein for the table.

The development of dual-purpose breeds created an economically viable option for the homesteader and the breeds remain an appealing option for the farmyard or self-sufficiency lifestyle.

CHARACTERISTICS

As all-rounders, dual-purpose breeds can fulfill the needs of most households. Many of the breeds tend to be less flighty than the layer breeds and they have the capacity to put on a reasonable amount of weight to provide meat for the table. While they do not reach the capability of the single-purpose breeds, they do provide a good balance between the two.

Dual-purpose breeds are durable and can be quick to trust the keeper, becoming tame over time. Their generally placid nature also makes them tolerant toward each other and to other breeds.

Breeding
There is a diversity of colors and feather types across the breeds, such as the stripes of the Amrock or the many varieties of Sussex, so mixing breeds together can create an attractive flock if there is no intention to breed.

If the intention is to breed, then it is important to note that some breeds within the group are nonsitters; however, those breeds that do become broody make excellent mothers who will rear almost any type of poultry as if their own.

Above *A pair of La Flèche displaying a well-rounded body form.*

Right *The Light Sussex is well known for its dual-purpose capabilities if the right bloodlines are acquired.*

CARE & MANAGEMENT

Dual-purpose breeds have a blend of needs from their mixed inheritance, so their care and management takes elements from both laying breeds and the heavier meat breeds. When establishing a care program, two things must be taken into account: the particular breed to be kept and the purpose of keeping it. For example, some breeds in this group are light enough to take to the wing and will, therefore, need a roofed-in run, whereas others tend toward the heavier build of the meat breeds and are easily contained behind a low fence.

Meat versus laying
If the intention is to use the poultry as a true dual-purpose breed, then space for growing stock needs to be taken into consideration. The birds intended for the table should be managed in a similar manner to the meat breeds; too much space to roam will result in the bird not putting on enough weight.

Those birds that are to be used for the laying flock should be given the chance to roam and forage for food. This is not only so that the birds can supplement their diet with natural foodstuffs, but also because it reduces the possibility of the birds becoming fat, thus lowering their laying capacity.

Sussex

ROOSTER WEIGHT
Large Fowl 9 lb. (4.1 kg)
Bantam 40 oz. (1.13 kg)

HEN WEIGHT
Large Fowl 7 lb. (3.2 kg)
Bantam 28 oz. (790 g)

COUNTRY/REGION OF ORIGIN
United Kingdom

Profile The Sussex has a long history and includes bloodlines that could be placed in either the table or the laying categories. It serves both functions well, making it predominantly a dual-purpose breed today. Initially developed in the nineteenth century, it is a heavy bird with a blocklike shape and comes in a variety of colors. Like the Rhode Island, it has played an important part in the development of today's commercial hybrids.

Behavior & upkeep The Sussex is a calm breed of chicken and can become friendly over time, being quick to trust its keeper. They tend to get along well with each other and, given enough space, it is possible to keep more than one male within a flock. A robust bird, it copes well with all weather conditions and is happy roaming free or within a fixed run. The hens are excellent layers, producing a good number of eggs even during the winter. They can become broody, and, if so, they are known to be good sitters and even better mothers.

COLOR
Plumage Light, white, silver, spangled, buff, red, brown
Eyes Dependent upon plumage; brown, red, or orange
Comb Single, evenly serrated **Feet & legs** Featherless, white

EGG COLOR Tinted

EGG PRODUCTION Medium to high

SHOW CLASSIFICATION Heavy; Soft Feather

Croad Langshan

ROOSTER WEIGHT
Large Fowl 9 lb. (4.1 kg)
Bantam 27–32 oz. (770–910 g)

HEN WEIGHT
Large Fowl 7 lb. (3.2 kg)
Bantam 23–28 oz. (650–710 g)

COUNTRY/REGION OF ORIGIN
China

COLOR
Plumage Black, white **Eyes** Brown
Comb Single, five or six serrations
Feet & legs Feathered (outer edge), blue/black

Profile A British Army major called Croad imported these birds into the United Kingdom in 1872. They reached the shores of the United States in 1898 and quickly established themselves as a useful dual-purpose breed, producing a good number of eggs plus a sizable bird for the table. Originally a black plumage bird, whites were developed but are infrequently encountered. A tall, upright stance combined with its weight gives the bird a striking and graceful appearance.

Behavior & upkeep Croad Langshans are strong and vigorous birds with an intelligent and inquisitive nature. They are docile and easily tamed by the keeper and tolerant toward others within a flock. Their heavy weight means they are unlikely to take to the wing and can be easily contained by a low fence. They are hardy birds that manage well in most weather conditions but, although their leg feathering is not profuse, care should be taken in muddy conditions.

EGG COLOR Brown, pinkish plum

EGG PRODUCTION Medium to high

SHOW CLASSIFICATION Heavy; Soft Feather

Ixworth

ROOSTER WEIGHT
Large Fowl 9 lb. (4.1 kg)
Bantam 36 oz. (1.02 kg)

HEN WEIGHT
Large Fowl 7 lb. (3.2 kg)
Bantam 28 oz. (790 g)

COUNTRY/REGION OF ORIGIN
United Kingdom

Profile The Ixworth is a sturdy-looking bird with a long but compact body. It was developed by Reginald Appleyard (of Appleyard duck fame) in the 1930s. Designed to appeal to homesteaders in the United Kingdom, it makes a good laying bird with excellent table qualities, including white skin and flesh. Created from a vast variety of breeds, its success was cut short by the appearance of function-specific hybrids within the commercial sector. It is now considered a rare breed, but still has a small dedicated following.

Behavior & upkeep Designed to function well on a homestead, this breed makes a great forager, capable of handling most climates and ideally suited for free roaming. Confinement can result in reduced laying ability and fatty birds. Despite its heavy size, it has strong wings and is capable of getting off the ground, so good fencing or a roofed-in run is needed. Cautious by nature, they can be tamed but do not make good pets. Good bloodlines can produce heavy-laying hens. They rarely sit, but if they do turn broody, they make good mothers.

COLOR
Plumage White **Eyes** Red, bright orange
Comb Pea **Feet & legs** Featherless, white

EGG COLOR Tinted

EGG PRODUCTION Medium to high

SHOW CLASSIFICATION Heavy; Rare

La Flèche

ROOSTER WEIGHT
Large Fowl 8–9 lb. (3.6–4.1 kg)
Bantam 36 oz. (1.02 kg)

HEN WEIGHT
Large Fowl 6–7 lb. (2.7–3.2 kg)
Bantam 28 oz. (800 g)

COUNTRY/REGION OF ORIGIN
France

Profile The combination of deep red, horned comb, strong beak, cavernous nostrils, and beetle-black plumage coupled with the solid stature of this breed makes it well suited to its nickname of "Satan's Fowl." It is a good layer but also grows quickly to quite a large size, making it an excellent table bird well known in its country of origin.

Behavior & upkeep La Flèche birds flourish best when they are allowed to roam freely; they are excellent foragers and will cover large distances in search of food. This makes them an economical breed, ideally suited to their dual-purpose function. They are also capable of flying high despite their size, so they need high fences or roofed areas if they are not to be found roosting in trees. Wary by nature, they do not tame easily, although they are not an aggressive breed.

COLOR
Plumage Black **Eyes** Red or black
Comb Double spike **Feet & legs** Clean, dark slate, or black

EGG COLOR White

EGG PRODUCTION Medium to high

SHOW CLASSIFICATION Heavy; Rare

Game Breeds

HISTORY

Game breeds originated in Asia and have a long history. They were introduced to satisfy the interest in cockfighting that has been popular throughout history. Because they were developed originally for their fighting ability, they share a number of key features but also appear in a diverse number of colors and shapes.

Now that cockfighting has largely been outlawed, game breeds today compete in the exhibition scene. Here, they are judged on their characteristics and posture as opposed to any of their physical abilities; feather coloring is a secondary consideration.

Game breeds have played an important part in the development of other breeds and breed types; careful observation of a breed, such as the Brahma, will indicate just how much influence they have had, particularly within the meat and ornamental groups.

Above *A painting of brown-breasted red game in the late nineteenth century.*

CHARACTERISTICS

The overriding characteristic of game breeds is their self-confidence. This can make them intolerant of other breeds and, in some cases, of other individuals within their breed or even their family group. They can, however, become extremely tame and trusting toward their keeper and are not known for flighty behavior. Their general appearance is one of dominance and strength, either exhibited in a squat, stocky posture or more often in a tall, upright presence.

Game breeds are known as "hard-feathered" breeds, meaning that the feathering is close to the body and absent in places, such as the breastbone. They rarely exhibit any form of ornamental feathering but do come in a vast array of color combinations.

In most cases, the wattles and combs are significantly reduced in size, which, combined with their facial skin folds and hooded brow, accentuates their menacing but unique appearance.

Egg laying
During the development of these breeds, egg-laying capacity was not considered a valuable attribute. Game breeds, therefore, remain poor layers today. However, many of the breeds do sit and will brood eggs; they make excellent mothers who will defend their offspring with ferocity.

CARE & MANAGEMENT

Game breeds do need particularly careful consideration if they are to be kept successfully. Each breed group, and, in many cases, the breeds within that group, will require an element of special management.

The history and development of game breeds means they can—and will—seek to be aggressive toward any bird that is not part of the flock. This is also true if birds are removed or added to the flock, so maintaining a stable group of individuals is essential if fights are to be avoided. Some of the breeds in this group are monogamous, so accommodation for only pairs will be required.

Conditions
Both the males and females are strong, powerful birds and adequate space is required for exercise. Also, because of their upright carriage, they benefit from having feeders suspended well above the ground and greens hanging just out of reach, encouraging the birds to stretch and jump for them.

They are by nature hardy breeds, comfortable in extremes of weather. Providing there is a dry, draft-free place for them to roost at night, they will flourish in most conditions.

Modern Game

ROOSTER WEIGHT
Large Fowl 7–9 lb. (3.2–4.1 kg)
Bantam 20–22 oz. (570–620 g)

HEN WEIGHT
Large Fowl 5–7 lb. (2.25–3.2 kg)
Bantam 16–18 oz. (450–510 g)

COUNTRY/REGION OF ORIGIN
United Kingdom

Profile The Modern Game breed came into being shortly after the 1849 ban on cockfighting in Great Britain. Breeders were more interested in looks than fighting qualities and, as a consequence, Modern Game birds came to have accentuated features with long, slender legs and an elongated neck. With a vast array of possible plumage colors and unusually profuse feathering for a tightly feathered breed, these birds look entirely at home in the exhibition and show arenas.

Behavior & upkeep As with most game breeds, the Modern Game will become trusting toward its keeper, but, unlike the others, its fighting spirit has become subdued by show breeding. They are, therefore, more tolerant toward each other, and happy to be part of a mixed flock, which makes accommodating them much simpler. They are hardy and cope well with most climates. The hens are poor layers and only do so for a few months a year. They can turn broody, but their shape and tight feathering don't make them ideal sitters.

COLOR Plumage Black, blue, white, blue/red, silver blue, lemon blue, black/red, brown/red, duckwing (gold, silver) (not shown: birchen, pyle, wheaten) **Eyes** Dependent on plumage **Comb** Single, small **Feet & legs** Featherless, color dependent upon plumage

EGG COLOR Tinted

EGG PRODUCTION Low

SHOW CLASSIFICATION Hard Feather

Ko Shamo

ROOSTER WEIGHT
Bantam 36 oz. (1 kg)

HEN WEIGHT
Bantam 28 oz. (800 g)

COUNTRY/REGION OF ORIGIN
Japan

Profile Ko Shamo means "little fighter" in Japanese. A diminutive derivative of the Shamo breed, it has a long history but didn't reach Europe until the late twentieth century. As a solid-looking little bird with an upright stance and tight but sparse feathering, it carries all the hallmarks of a game breed. The breastbone is often unfeathered; along with the stumpy tail, this can give the bird an unkempt look to the untrained eye.

Behavior & upkeep Ko Shamo birds live up to their name. They are extremely intolerant of other birds, both of the same and different breeds. A keeper must pay close attention when establishing breeding groups; any more than one rooster from the age of six weeks onward, or any unbalancing of an existing flock, can result in serious fighting between the birds. Despite this, the birds respond well to close and regular contact with their keeper and can become tame. They are extremely hardy and cope easily with poor weather conditions, but the hens are poor layers and only do so for a short period of time each year.

COLOR Plumage Black, black/red, black mottled, blue, buff, duckwing, gray, white, cuckoo (not shown: spangled)
Eyes Pearl or yellow **Comb** Pea, walnut, or chrysanthemum
Feet & legs Featherless, yellow, dusky on dark plumaged varieties

EGG COLOR Tinted or cream

EGG PRODUCTION Low

SHOW CLASSIFICATION Hard Feather; Rare

Malay

ROOSTER WEIGHT
Large Fowl 11 lb. (5 kg)
Bantam 42–48 oz. (1.19–1.36 kg)

HEN WEIGHT
Large Fowl 9 lb. (4.1 kg)
Bantam 36–40 oz. (1.02–1.13 kg)

COUNTRY/REGION OF ORIGIN
Asia

Profile A ramrod-straight bearing and gaunt features combine to give Malay chickens a fierce appearance. They arrived in Europe in the 1830s, descendants of a giant fowl that is now extinct. Breeders have since sought to accentuate their height (they can stand over 3 feet/90 cm tall), posture, and shape for the show pen. Stout-skulled, tight-feathered, and hard-muscled, they display all the attributes of game birds and have played an important role in the development of many more-modern poultry breeds.

Behavior & upkeep As might be expected with such powerfully built birds, Malays can be extremely headstrong. They will trust their keeper and can become tame, but they will treat other birds and animals with suspicion, and both sexes will attack. To avoid problems, they should be kept in pairs or trios. They are robust and hardy birds, more than equipped to handle extremes of weather; the roost needs only to be dry and draft-free. Like other game breeds, Malay hens are not good layers and usually only do so for a couple of months a year.

COLOR
Plumage Black, black/red, white, spangled, pyle
Eyes White, yellow, pearl, or "daw"(pearl-colored like a jackdaw)
Comb Small half-walnut **Feet & legs** Featherless, yellow

EGG COLOR Tinted

EGG PRODUCTION Low

SHOW CLASSIFICATION Hard Feather; Rare

Indian Game/Cornish

ROOSTER WEIGHT
Large Fowl 8 lb. (3.6 kg)
Bantam 4½ lb. (2 kg)

HEN WEIGHT
Large Fowl 6 lb. (2.7 kg)
Bantam 3½ lb. (1.5 kg)

COUNTRY/REGION OF ORIGIN
United Kingdom

Profile This squat and wide-legged breed was developed using imported Asils in the English counties of Devon and Cornwall, hence the alternative name of "Cornish." Originally intended as an improvement on the English game fowl breeds of the late eighteenth century, they were soon also put to use in the development of table breeds. Solid and thickset with a beetled brow, an Indian Game chicken has a menacing look about it.

Behavior & upkeep Although developed from fighting breeds, Indian Game chickens can be friendly toward their keeper, but not toward other animals or birds—including each other. They should generally be kept in groups of no more than two. Their weight means that flight is out of the question, so low fencing is sufficient. They are an extremely tough breed, but their hard feathers are prone to breaking, which can affect the look of the bird. They benefit from roaming freely but can be kept in a smaller space as long as care is taken that they do not get fat. The hens tend to lay few eggs—usually only during the spring.

COLOR
Plumage Dark, jubilee, double-laced blue
Eyes Pale red or pearl **Comb** Pea, red
Feet & legs Featherless, rich orange, or deep yellow

EGG COLOR Tinted

EGG PRODUCTION Low

SHOW CLASSIFICATION Heavy; Hard Feather

Laying Breeds

HISTORY

Up until fairly recent times, almost all domesticated chickens were viewed as egg layers. The primary purpose of the chicken was to lay eggs, and a lot of them. Only when the bird ceased being productive would it be culled and used to provide meat for the table.

Many countries and regions carefully developed their own breeds specifically suited to their local environment. Consequently, there is a wide range of laying breeds with a long history; some, such as the Lakenvelder, date back to the early eighteenth century, and others, such as the New Hampshire, emerged as a breed only in the early twentieth century.

Unfortunately for the pure laying breeds, it was during the first half of the twentieth century that the modern hybrid layer appeared within the poultry world and went on to take command of the commercial egg market as it is today.

CHARACTERISTICS

Chickens that fall within the egg-laying category are usually smaller in size than those that are bred for meat or sit within the dual-purpose category. The reason is simple; they put their energies into laying eggs and not into putting on body mass. They also tend to begin laying sooner than the other types of chicken; the idea being to have them reach maturity by twenty weeks of age, and to lay as many eggs as possible within the first few years.

Laying breeds are often excellent foragers, scratching and digging

Below *A pair of New Hampshire Reds now best known for their laying capability.*

Above *Laying breeds are nonsitters which means that they don't tend to go broody.*

CARE & MANAGEMENT

The laying breeds tend to be lighter in body, more agile, and in most cases quite capable of short flight. As such, high fences or roofed-in runs are required to stop them straying too far if free roaming is not an option. They are predominantly clean-legged so cope well on wetter ground or muddier conditions than those with foot feathering. The breeds are designed to lay daily for as long as daylight hours allow and this can equate to 280+ eggs in the first year.

It is good management practice to weed out poor-performing individuals within a flock if there is an intention to breed replacements. Birds that have good feathering toward the end of the season or ones still laying eggs with heavy pigmentation are infrequent layers and should not be bred from.

industriously for additional titbits. This trait contributes toward the group's efficiency by minimizing the feed costs for maximum output. Their nature is sprightly although shy, and they can be wary of their keepers, who need to show a patient and relaxed approach if they are to successfully tame the birds.

Laying breeds also fall into the "nonsitting" category, meaning that they rarely turn broody. Broodiness is a trait not favored in layers, and over the centuries it has been selected out through careful breeding.

Bloodlines

It is important to note that the output of a particular chicken can depend on the bloodline the bird comes from. Many of the breeds—or colors within a breed—that were once excellent layers have changed over the years, and although the breed may remain visually the same, some are now developed for exhibition; check before purchasing stock.

If the intention is to raise laying breeds from fertile eggs, alternative hatching methods will be needed, such as an artificial incubator or a willing broody hen of a different breed.

Leghorn

ROOSTER WEIGHT
Large Fowl 7½ lb. (3.4 kg)
Bantam 36 oz. (1.02 kg)

HEN WEIGHT
Large Fowl 5½ lb. (2.5 kg)
Bantam 32 oz. (910 g)

COUNTRY/REGION OF ORIGIN
Mediterranean

Profile The Leghorn has played a major part in the development of today's egg-producing hybrids. Originally thought to originate from Italy, it has been bred along discrete lines in a number of countries—notably in North America since the 1870s. This has led to a significant diversity in country "standards," although some similarities do remain. Initially, it was a much lighter bird, but it is thought that crosses with Malay and Minorca have given it extra weight.

Behavior & upkeep This breed is an excellent forager, copes well with free roaming, and is robust enough to deal with poor weather conditions. The birds can be kept within the confines of a run, but high fencing or a roof will be needed because they are capable of flight, often choosing a tree to roost in as opposed to a henhouse. Their large headgear is prone to become dry or frostbitten in cold weather; the application of petroleum jelly can help prevent this. However, they are not prone to broodiness, so an incubator or another broody breed will be required to hatch new stock.

COLOR Plumage Black, brown, white, buff, duckwing (silver and gold), exchequer, cuckoo, mottled, pyle **Eyes** Red
Comb Single (erect in male, fallen in female) or rose
Feet & legs Featherless, yellow or orange

EGG COLOR White

EGG PRODUCTION High

SHOW CLASSIFICATION Light; Soft Feather

Orpington

ROOSTER WEIGHT
Large Fowl 10 lb. (4.55 kg)
Bantam 3¾ lb. (1.7 kg)

HEN WEIGHT
Large Fowl 7½ lb. (3.4 kg)
Bantam 3¼ lb. (1.5 kg)

COUNTRY/REGION OF ORIGIN
United Kingdom

Profile Named after the English village in which it was developed in 1886, the Orpington was initially hailed for its incredible laying qualities. Today, the bird is still capable of laying a good number of eggs but not to such an outstanding degree. The breed is well represented on the exhibition circuit and comes in a vast array of colors. Immense in size and profusely feathered, Orpingtons are extremely popular with poultry keepers.

Behavior & upkeep The Orpington is a large, broad bird that requires suitably spacious accommodation. They are equally happy to live in a run or to roam freely, and because their size makes them less inclined to fly, they can easily be contained behind a low fence. They manage well in most conditions, but in wet weather their mass of soft feathering can easily become soaked; it is essential to provide sheltered areas, where they can dry off. Friendly and easy to tame, they will quickly trust their keeper and make rewarding pets. The hens lay well and can become broody, going on to make reliable mothers for their offspring.

COLOR Plumage Black, blue, buff, white, gold laced, silver laced, jubilee, red, mottled (not shown: birchen, splash, partridge)
Eyes Dependent on plumage **Comb** Single, small, evenly serrated
Feet & legs Featherless, color dependent on plumage

EGG COLOR Tinted to brown

EGG PRODUCTION Medium to high

SHOW CLASSIFICATION Heavy; Soft Feather

Wyandotte

ROOSTER WEIGHT
Large Fowl 9 lb. (4.08 kg)
Bantam 3.75 lb. (1.70 kg)

HEN WEIGHT
Large Fowl 7 lb. (3.17 kg)
Bantam 3 lb. (1.36 kg)

COUNTRY/REGION OF ORIGIN
North America

Profile It is not entirely clear which breeds were used to create the Wyandotte, but it is generally held that Cochins played a significant part. Initially, the breed was available in the silver-laced variety and this was the first to be standardized back in 1883 in the United States. Today, after a series of crosses into a number of breeds, it is possible to see Wyandottes in a wide range of colors. They are heavy-looking birds, but this is partly due to their profusion of soft feathering.

Behavior & upkeep Wyandottes are strong and vigorous birds that cope well in a confined run or free roaming. They are capable of taking to the wing but are not eager flyers; a low fence is usually enough to hold them. They are trusting birds and quickly become friendly, which makes them ideal as pets or for young children. The hens lay a good number of eggs but are extremely prone to turn broody. They make good mothers, but their broodiness needs to be discouraged to avoid deterioration in the condition of the hens.

COLOR
Plumage Black, blue, buff, white, red, silver, barred, Columbian, partridge (not shown: laced (silver, blue, gold, buff), penciled)
Eyes Orange or red **Comb** Rose **Feet & legs** Featherless, yellow

EGG COLOR Tinted to brown

EGG PRODUCTION Medium to high

SHOW CLASSIFICATION Heavy; Soft Feather

Rhode Island

ROOSTER WEIGHT
Large Fowl 8 lb. (3.6 kg)
Bantam 28–32 oz. (790–910 g)

HEN WEIGHT
Large Fowl 6 lb. (3.8 kg)
Bantam 24–28 oz. (680–790 g)

COUNTRY/REGION OF ORIGIN
North America

Profile The Rhode Island, or "Rhodie," is possibly the best-known and most influential breed of chicken in recent times. Developed originally as a dual-purpose breed, it became famous for its role in the creation of commercial laying strains. It is mostly seen in its red form; a Rhode Island White was developed but never became globally popular and is rarely seen outside of the United States these days. Described as "brick shaped," this is a solid breed that will still serve the table well.

Behavior & upkeep As befitting a laying breed, Rhode Island hens can lay an average of 250 eggs per year. This makes them useful for both small- and large-scale keepers. They tend to be calm around keepers and have little desire to take to the wing so can be kept in an enclosed run. They are equally good as free roamers, with excellent foraging skills. The chicks grow fast and pullets can be in lay by twenty weeks. They are also hardy birds well adapted to extremes of climate. This combination of attributes makes them a great breed for beginners.

COLOR
Plumage Deep red **Eyes** Red
Comb Single or rose
Feet & legs Featherless; yellow or red horn

EGG COLOR Light brown
EGG PRODUCTION High
SHOW CLASSIFICATION Heavy; Soft Feather

Plymouth Rock

ROOSTER WEIGHT
Large Fowl 7½ lb. (3.4 kg)
Bantam 3 lb. (1.36 kg)

HEN WEIGHT
Large Fowl 6½ lb. (2.95 kg)
Bantam 2½ lb. (1.13 kg)

COUNTRY/REGION OF ORIGIN
North America

Profile The Plymouth Rock was created during the 1860s and 1870s using a combination predominantly made up of the Brahma, Java, Dominique, and Cochin breeds. The objective was to create a heavy, vigorous bird with excellent laying qualities. The Barred variety was the first to be standardized in the early 1870s and, at around the same time, the breed was exported to Europe. Originally known as the Barred Plymouth Rock, other colors were developed and the term "barred" was dropped from the name.

Behavior & upkeep This breed can manage well in confinement but prefers free-roaming conditions. They are simple to keep—robust enough to cope with extremes of weather and rarely taking to the wing. Placid by nature, they become tame easily and make a friendly addition to a flock. The roosters are tolerant and—with enough space—more than one can be kept in a flock. The hens lay well and can turn broody, making attentive mothers.

COLOR
Plumage Black, white, buff, barred, Columbian
Eyes Bay to red **Comb** Single, medium, even serrations
Feet & legs Featherless, yellow

EGG COLOR Tinted

EGG PRODUCTION Medium to high

SHOW CLASSIFICATION Heavy; Soft Feather

New Hampshire Red

ROOSTER WEIGHT
Large Fowl 8½ lb. (3.85 kg)
Bantam 34 oz. (980 g)

HEN WEIGHT
Large Fowl 6½ lb. (2.95 kg)
Bantam 26 oz. (737 g)

COUNTRY/REGION OF ORIGIN
United States

Profile Developed in the state of New Hampshire during the early twentieth century, this breed was built predominantly from Rhode Island birds. Its primary focus has always been egg production, but it is nevertheless a good bird for the table. New Hampshire Reds quickly became popular in their home country, but it was not until the 1940s that they gained any kind of following in Europe, where they remain a rare breed.

Behavior & upkeep This is a hardy breed that thrives in both a free-roaming and more confined environment. Despite its weight, it is capable of some flight; a fence of 5 feet (1.5 m) should be sufficient to keep them contained. They are friendly and tolerant of their own and other breeds. The roosters, too, are not aggressive and can be easily tamed. They are fast growing and it is possible with the right bloodline to run the flock for dual purposes. The hens lay a good number of eggs, although broodiness is not a common trait.

COLOR
Plumage Chestnut red **Eyes** Bay
Comb Single, medium, five well-defined points
Feet & legs Featherless, yellow with a red tinge

EGG COLOR Tinted to brown

EGG PRODUCTION Medium to high

SHOW CLASSIFICATION Heavy; Rare

Welsummer

ROOSTER WEIGHT
Large Fowl 7 lb. (3.2 kg)
Bantam 36 oz. (1.02 kg)

HEN WEIGHT
Large Fowl 6 lb. (2.7 kg)
Bantam 28 oz. (790 g)

COUNTRY/REGION OF ORIGIN
Netherlands

Profile Developed in and named after the Dutch village of Welsum, this breed was constructed from a wide variety of birds, including the Brahma, Malay, Orpington, Leghorn, and Wyandotte. It was standardized by the Dutch in the mid-1920s and then exported to other countries from the 1930s onward. Famed for its capacity to lay deep brown eggs, it can be a heavy breed despite being categorized as "Light" in some countries.

Behavior & upkeep Their famously brown eggs and rich, warmly colored feathering make Welsummers very desirable birds to keep. They are excellent foragers, ideally suited to a free-roam environment but capable of coping with confinement. In either case, some fencing will be required given that they are capable of flight over short distances. They have an active nature and will gradually become trusting of their keeper. The hens lay well but less so during the winter months. They can turn broody but keepers looking to rear productive young need to make sure that they are breeding from good layers.

COLOR
Plumage Partridge, duckwing (silver) **Eyes** Red
Comb Single, medium, five to seven serrations
Feet & legs Featherless, yellow

EGG COLOR Brown to deep brown

EGG PRODUCTION Medium to high

SHOW CLASSIFICATION Light; Soft Feather

Barnevelder

ROOSTER WEIGHT
Large Fowl 7–8 lb. (3.2–3.6 kg)
Bantam 32 oz. (910 g)

HEN WEIGHT
Large Fowl 6–7 lb. (2.7–3.2 kg)
Bantam 26 oz. (740 g)

COUNTRY/REGION OF ORIGIN
Netherlands

Profile Named after the Dutch town of Barneveld, where it was created, this is a brown-egg-laying breed thought to have been developed from a combination of breeds, including Cochins, Brahmas, and Langshans. It was exported to the United Kingdom around 1900 and, from there, on to other countries. Although other plumage types are seen, it is perhaps best known for the intricate double-laced variety. Its beautiful dark brown eggs help to make it an attractive breed to keep.

Behavior & upkeep Barnevelders are an average size and not prone to flying, but they can jump well, so a medium-size fence should be used to keep them contained. Happy to roam freely or to be housed in an enclosure, they have a placid nature and will become tame if handled calmly. The hens are good layers and can turn broody but are not noted for this. Unfortunately, the breed is susceptible to Marek's disease; vaccinated stock should always be purchased. Vaccination should also be considered if breeding is an objective.

 COLOR
Plumage Black, double-laced, partridge **Eyes** Orange
Comb Single, medium **Feet & legs** Featherless, yellow

EGG COLOR Brown

EGG PRODUCTION Medium to high

SHOW CLASSIFICATION Heavy; Soft Feather

Araucana

ROOSTER WEIGHT
Large Fowl 6–7 lb. (2.7–3.2 kg)
Bantam 26–30 oz. (740–850 g)

HEN WEIGHT
Large Fowl 5–6 lb. (2.2–2.7 kg)
Bantam 24–28 oz. (680–790 g)

COUNTRY/REGION OF ORIGIN
Chile

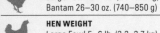

Profile This is a majestic breed well known for its bearded appearance, thanks to the thick muffling it sports around the ears and throat. The breed originates from Chile and it is believed its name Araucana is derived from the Arauca province in the north of the country, where the indigenous peoples were never conquered by the Spaniards. The birds we see today were standardized in Scotland in the 1930s by George Malcolm, who created the first true, breeding, lavender-colored Araucanas.

Behavior & upkeep Araucanas are vigorous and hardy birds that handle poor weather conditions with ease. They are prolific layers of blue or green eggs, which are unique for the way in which their color permeates throughout the shell. The hens are infrequent brooders, but, when they do sit, they make good mothers. As a crested breed, ideally they should not be mixed with noncrested varieties, because their vision can be slightly impaired, making them vulnerable to bullying attacks.

COLOR Plumage Lavender, black/red, blue, silver or gold duckwing, black/blue, white, cuckoo, black (not shown: spangled, pyle, crele) **Eyes** Dark orange **Comb** Small pea **Feet & legs** Featherless, willow to slate (except cuckoo variety)

EGG COLOR Blue or green

EGG PRODUCTION Medium to high

SHOW CLASSIFICATION Soft Feather; Light

Marans

ROOSTER WEIGHT
Large Fowl 7–8 lb. (3.2–3.6 kg)
Bantam 28–32 oz. (790–910 g)

HEN WEIGHT
Large Fowl 6–7 lb. (2.7–3.2 kg)
Bantam 24–28 oz. (680–790 g)

COUNTRY/REGION OF ORIGIN
France

Profile This breed takes its name from the town of Marans in France and its heritage comes from a variety of breeds, such as Croad Langshan and Faverolles. Originally developed as a dual-purpose breed, it is now mostly kept for its laying capability and the intense chocolate-brown eggs that certain lines can produce. A sizable bird with a long carriage, the breed comes in two distinct groups: the English Marans, which has no feathers on its legs, and the French Marans, which does.

Behavior & upkeep Marans can be curious and will approach the keeper with interest, but they rarely allow themselves to be touched and do not become tame easily. These vigorous birds are well suited to a free-roaming lifestyle but can also be kept within a run. The feathering on the French Marans' legs is less profuse than on other feather-legged breeds, so they can cope with muddy conditions. The hens lay a good number of eggs and— although they are not known for their sitting—some do turn broody.

COLOR
Plumage Black, cuckoo **Eyes** Red or bright orange
Comb Single, medium, five to seven serrations
Feet & legs Featherless, white

EGG COLOR Dark brown

EGG PRODUCTION Medium to high

SHOW CLASSIFICATION Heavy; Soft Feather

Ancona

ROOSTER WEIGHT
Large Fowl 6 lb. (2.7 kg)
Bantam 20–24 oz. (570–680 g)

HEN WEIGHT
Large Fowl 5 lb. (2.25 kg)
Bantam 18–22 oz. (510–620 g)

COUNTRY/REGION OF ORIGIN
Italy

Profile This breed originated in the town of Ancona in central Italy. It was first imported to Great Britain in the 1850s and then to North America during the latter half of the same century. There is some controversy surrounding its closeness in appearance and manner to the Leghorn, but it is officially regarded as a separate breed. It has its own dedicated following, attracted particularly by its laying ability.

Behavior & upkeep Anconas are active birds with excellent foraging skills, best suited to a free-roaming environment. They are correspondingly unlikely to be tamed or trained to the hand. They are excellent flyers and will easily clear low fencing, so roofing or high fencing is required to keep them contained. They are tolerant of most climates and need little in terms of special care. The hens are excellent layers. In fact, they were many people's laying breed of choice prior to the arrival of specialty hybrids. They are considered nonsitters and rarely turn broody.

COLOR
Plumage Black (green beetling) with white "V" tip to feathers
Eyes Orange, red **Comb** Single (medium, five to seven serrations) or rose
Feet & legs Featherless, yellow with black mottling

EGG COLOR White or cream
EGG PRODUCTION High
SHOW CLASSIFICATION Light; Soft Feather

Australlorp

ROOSTER WEIGHT
Large Fowl 8½–10 lb. (3.8–4.5 kg)
Bantam 36 oz. (1.02 kg)

HEN WEIGHT
Large Fowl 6½–8 lb. (2.9–3.6 kg)
Bantam 28 oz. (790 g)

COUNTRY/REGION OF ORIGIN
Australia

Profile This breed's name betrays its history as an Australian development of the English Orpington chicken. It was designed during the early twentieth century with maximum utility in mind. It is a good layer and sufficiently sizable and quick growing to suit the table. It is now found the world over, both as a utility breed and on the exhibition circuit.

Behavior & upkeep Australorp birds are lively and active but also mild mannered and reasonably easy to tame. They are tolerant to each other and toward other breeds. The roosters are not known for aggression and it is perfectly possible to rear young males together without fighting occurring. Their size means they have a limited ability to get off the ground; a normal-height fence will be sufficient to contain them. A hardy breed, the Australorp copes with most weather conditions and is happy free roaming or in a fixed run. The hens are good layers and rarely turn broody.

COLOR
Plumage Black, blue, white **Eyes** Black
Comb Single, medium, four to six serrations
Feet & legs Featherless, black

EGG COLOR Tinted to brown
EGG PRODUCTION Medium to high
SHOW CLASSIFICATION Heavy; Soft Feather

Meat Breeds

HISTORY

Meat breeds are often more politely referred to as "table" breeds; they were developed with the primary aim of providing meat for the table. Surplus roosters from many of the laying breeds proved too lightweight to supply a practical source of meat, and while the dual-purpose, or utility, breeds straddled the line well in terms of fulfilling the need for eggs and meat, neither gained weight quickly enough to be considered an effective source of inexpensive meat.

Originally, meat breeds came about due to unintentional matings between different breeds that occasionally resulted in fast-growing, heavyweight offspring. Careful selection of these larger offspring and additional breeding then resulted in consistently weighty results.

After World War II, many of these breeds became obsolete, thanks to the emergence of table hybrids designed to meet increasing demand for cheap protein; however, some can still be found on small-scale farms and homesteads.

Above *The Faverolles is a popular option as a table breed.*

CHARACTERISTICS

Meat breed chickens are heavy and large, with the males of some breeds weighing in at over 11 pounds (5 kg). The hens are not too far behind, which means that both sexes are highly suitable for use in the kitchen. However, this may make them an unsuitable choice if small children will be involved in looking after them.

On the other hand, table breeds tend to be more placid and slow-moving birds; a breed that is active and flighty will not put on weight so quickly. They are also tolerant and not prone to aggression toward each other or their keeper.

Meat breed chickens tend to be characterized by a more full-chested profile; a good deal of their weight gain is carried on the breast, shifting the bird's center of gravity forward.

Egg laying
The development of these birds for meat means that little attention was paid to their laying qualities; some are, therefore, relatively poor layers when compared with those developed for egg production. Meat breeds do, however, show a greater propensity toward brooding than the laying types, with the hens making excellent mothers. Their size also means that they are capable of hatching large clutches of eggs.

CARE & MANAGEMENT

The majority of meat breeds do not readily take to the wing and can be kept behind relatively low fencing. In fact, their general docility and low mobility is such that they will happily live within a penned space as opposed to needing large areas over which to roam.

Feeding and exercise
Due to their size and nature, they can have quite an appetite and it is important to be sure that they are adequately fed. They must not, however, be overfed or given foodstuffs too rich in calories; this can lead to the birds becoming fat and, if left unchecked, result in leg problems. By the same measure, meat breeds need exercise to avoid becoming fat.

To keep your birds exercised within a small enclosure, hang greens just out of reach so that the bird has to stretch and jump slightly to access the fodder.

Accommodation
Due to the large size of meat breeds, their accommodation needs to be given careful consideration. Entrance holes need to be large enough for them to enter and exit the house easily, the nest boxes need to be large enough for the hens to sit comfortably without causing damage to their plumage, and perches should not be situated too far off floor level to reduce the risk of leg injuries when they alight.

Faverolles

ROOSTER WEIGHT
Large Fowl 9–11 lb. (4–5 kg)
Bantam 3 lb. (1.36 kg)

HEN WEIGHT
Large Fowl 7–9 lb. (3–4 kg)
Bantam 2 lb. (900 g)

COUNTRY/REGION OF ORIGIN
France

Profile Faverolles have a deep, heavy-looking, long build, indicative of their table heritage. Their feathered legs and beard give them a striking presence within a mixed flock. The original color of Faverolles chicks is salmon—a background coloration that makes it easier to discern the differences in plumage that denote male and female chicks. Originating around the mid-nineteenth century, Faverolles were bred using mainly Brahmas and Dorkings, and they share a number of the characteristics of these two fowl.

Behavior & upkeep These are friendly, docile, and gentle birds that seem to enjoy the company of their keepers. They are happy within a run and do not roam far, but they will grow fat if not given enough exercise. They are nonflyers and a low fence will keep them confined. With limited leg feathering, they are hardy and capable of handling poor weather. The hens lay a reasonable number of eggs and are known to continue in winter. They are nonsitters and seldom turn broody. The cocks are tolerant of each other and are rarely aggressive.

COLOR Plumage: Black, blue laced, buff, cuckoo, ermine, salmon, white **Eyes** Black, brown, orange, gray, hazel—depending on plumage **Comb** Single, medium size, upright, four to six serrations **Feet & legs** Sparsely feathered, five toes

EGG COLOR Tinted

EGG PRODUCTION Medium

SHOW CLASSIFICATION Heavy; Soft Feather

Dorking

ROOSTER WEIGHT
Large Fowl 10–14 lb. (4.5–6.3 kg)
Bantam 40–48 oz. (1.13–1.36 kg)

HEN WEIGHT
Large Fowl 8–10 lb. (3.6–4.5 kg)
Bantam 32–40 oz. (910–1.13 kg)

COUNTRY/REGION OF ORIGIN
United Kingdom

Profile The Dorking is an ancient breed believed to descend from similar five-toed birds described in texts written in 47 CE about Roman Britain. It is an extremely heavy bird but, in contrast to other giant chickens, no evidence has yet been found linking it to the huge breeds known to have originated in Asia. Well established in the early nineteenth century, it made a significant contribution to the development of other table breeds.

Behavior & upkeep Spacious housing is required to accommodate the Dorking's huge size and loose feathering. In contrast, they do not need much in terms of outdoor space and are content within a fixed run. However, care must be taken to avoid them becoming fat through lack of exercise. They can become tame, if handled calmly, but their size makes them less than ideal pets. The hens tend to lay only during the spring and summer, and low fertility rates can present a challenge for anyone wanting to breed from a flock.

COLOR
Plumage Silver gray, red, white, dark, cuckoo **Eyes** Bright red
Comb Single, large, or rose **Feet & legs** Featherless, five toes

EGG COLOR Tinted

EGG PRODUCTION Low to medium

SHOW CLASSIFICATION Heavy; Soft Feather

Jersey Giant

ROOSTER WEIGHT
Large Fowl 13 lb. (5.9 kg)
Bantam 3¼ lb. (1.74 kg)

HEN WEIGHT
Large Fowl 10 lb. (4.55 kg)
Bantam 2½ lb. (1.13 kg)

COUNTRY/REGION OF ORIGIN
North America

COLOR
Plumage Black, blue, white **Eyes** Brown, black
Comb Single, six even serrations
Feet & legs Featherless, willow

Profile This huge breed of chicken dates back to the 1880s, when it was created as a table breed in New Jersey. It was developed through the crossing of breeds, such as the Brahma, Croad Langshan, and Java fowl, and records from the early twentieth century give examples weighing in excess of 20 pounds (9 kg) (although these were usually caponized males). It is a broad and deep-shape bird originally only available in black. In recent years, other colors have come to the fore.

Behavior & upkeep By nature, Jersey Giants are calm and tolerant of each other and of other breeds. However, their bulk makes them difficult to handle, especially for children; they also require appropriate-size housing and a good amount of space in which to roam. On the other hand, their weight means that they do not fly and a low fence will contain them. The hens are reasonable layers and their eggs are a good size. The chicks grow quickly, but they take some time to reach their full-grown weight.

EGG COLOR Tinted or brown

EGG PRODUCTION Medium

SHOW CLASSIFICATION Heavy; Rare

North Holland Blue

ROOSTER WEIGHT
Large Fowl 8–10 lb. (3.6–4.6 kg)
Bantam 42 oz. (1.19 kg)

HEN WEIGHT
Large Fowl 7–9 lb. (3.2–4.1 kg)
Bantam 36 oz. (1.02 kg)

COUNTRY/REGION OF ORIGIN
Netherlands

Profile These are big, heavy chickens with a rounded body structure and a deep, broad breast. They have pink skin and white flesh, which makes for an attractive color combination on the table. Developed in the early twentieth century to withstand the cold, wet climate of the Zaan region of North Holland, these birds were bred by crossing fast-growing breeds from Belgium with the local fowl.

Behavior & upkeep Fast growing and placid, North Holland Blues rarely take to the wing and can easily become tame. However, their huge size makes them unsuitable for small children. They are happy to roam freely but equally thrive in more confined conditions, providing that care is taken not to overfeed them. The breed is tolerant of its own and other breeds and does not usually exhibit aggression. The fact that Plymouth Rocks were used in the later development of the breed means that their laying capacity is reasonable, with hens producing around 130 eggs a year.

COLOR
Plumage Blue/gray barred **Eyes** Orange, red
Comb Single; five to seven neat serrations
Feet & legs Lightly feathered, blue shaded, or white

EGG COLOR Tinted

EGG PRODUCTION Medium

SHOW CLASSIFICATION Heavy; Rare

Ornamental Breeds

HISTORY

Although ornamental breeds do not appear to serve the same practical purpose as laying or meat breeds, they have played an important role in the history and evolution of chickens. Back in the late eighteenth and early nineteenth centuries, it became a custom for rich landowners to beautify their yards and property with expensive ornaments and plants.

As a means of showing off their wealth still further, they would also adorn their estates with exotic-looking breeds of chicken. As a result, many paintings from this era contain chickens, and these provide a valuable insight not only into the makeup and nature of the birds, but also the diversity of "fancy" breeds kept at that time.

Careful, selective breeding would take place in order to produce point-perfect poultry, their development driven to promote form over function, accentuating particular features to provide fascination and impact.

CHARACTERISTICS

It could be said that the only thing ornamental breeds have in common is that they do not sit easily within any of the other breed groups—layers, meat, game, and dual-purpose. This is not to say that they have different characteristics but that they only share some of the key aspects of those breed groups. Some are light and flighty and make excellent layers, others have strong game bird origins and attributes, while others, such as the Brahma, are huge docile birds that were at some time used for meat.

Features and appearance
What many of the breeds do have in common is that they carry hereditary features that are often unique to that specific breed, such as beards, feather pattern, or length of leg. It is, however, impossible to provide a general profile of this group of birds beyond saying that they are "showy." They often have a high-maintenance appearance and this can entail a labor of love for the keeper, but, if managed correctly, they can epitomize what it was like to keep and breed poultry during the "Hen Fever" of the nineteenth century.

CARE & MANAGEMENT

As the characteristics of individual ornamental breeds vary so dramatically, so do the husbandry programs that are needed. Because it is the look and condition of the birds' plumage that is in many respects the breeds' main function, care should focus on the maintenance of appearance.

Crested breeds need chest-level drinkers to avoid the risk of head feathers getting wet and dirty. Long-tailed breeds require housing that has enough space to accommodate either the profuse plumes of certain breeds, such as the Sumatra, or the length of trail typical of other breeds,

such as the Yokohama. Breeds with a feather type similar to the Silkie will survive the outdoors, but in poor weather their feathering will soon start to look out of condition. Exposure to the sun can soon cause discoloration for birds with white plumage, whereas certain birds, such as the Sultan—with its head crest, beard, and feathered legs—will need their accommodation and outdoor area carefully maintained.

For exhibitors of fancy chickens, looking after a bird's appearance is the main challenge, but with the right management, ornamental breeds really can be head turners.

Right *The profuse feathering on the heads of some ornamental breeds can be a challenge to keep tidy and free from parasites.*

Poland

ROOSTER WEIGHT
Large Fowl 6½ lb. (2.95 kg)
Bantam 24–28 oz. (680–790 g)

HEN WEIGHT
Large Fowl 5 lb. (2.25 kg)
Bantam 18–24 oz. (510–680 g)

COUNTRY/REGION OF ORIGIN
Eastern Europe

Profile The Poland is an extremely old breed, reported to have reached Europe as early as the Middle Ages. It was certainly one of the first to be standardized back in the 1840s. Its actual ancestry is not clear. Despite its name, it is not believed to have originated in Poland. Some believe that it has its roots in Eastern Europe, Russia or even farther east in Asia.

Behavior & upkeep Sprightly and active, Polands can be a little nervy, thanks to the large crest that obscures their vision. To avoid causing them unnecessary surprise, it is a good idea to make some noise as you approach and to keep your hands at their eye level. The crests themselves should be checked and treated regularly for lice, and a roofed-in run is necessary to keep them clean and tidy. The hens rarely turn broody, so another breed or incubator will be required if a rearing program is desired.

COLOR
Plumage Black, white, blue, silver, gold, chamois, white-crested black, cuckoo **Eyes** Red **Comb** Horn, very small
Feet & legs Blue or horn

EGG COLOR White

EGG PRODUCTION Medium

SHOW CLASSIFICATION Light; Soft Feather

Silkie

ROOSTER WEIGHT
Large Fowl 4 lb. (1.8 kg)
Bantam 22 oz. (600 g)

HEN WEIGHT
Large Fowl 3 lb. (1.35 kg)
Bantam 18 oz. (500 g)

COUNTRY/REGION OF ORIGIN
Asia

Profile The Silkie is one of the best-known and most commonly kept breeds of decorative chickens, and they are popular as pets. They have fine hairlike feathers, mulberry skin, and turquoise ears, giving them a most striking aspect. Their exact origin is under dispute, but they are undoubtedly an ancient breed—they were referred to as "furry chickens" by Marco Polo during his thirteenth-century exploration of China. Their distinctive appearance has also seen them marketed in years gone by as a cross between a rabbit and a chicken.

Behavior & upkeep Silkies can be a pleasure to own—docile, friendly, and quick to trust their keepers. Despite their delicate appearance, they are surprisingly hardy and tolerant of poor weather conditions. However, mud and rain can quickly make a mess of their unusual feathering, so shelter does need to be provided. The hens are not heavy layers but will provide around 100 eggs a year in ideal conditions. They also have a strong urge to turn broody, making them a popular choice for those who want to rear some chicks.

COLOR
Plumage Black, blue, white, gold, partridge; some bearded versions; distinctive feathering **Eyes** Black **Comb** Circular, mulberry color **Feet & legs** Feathered legs, five toes

EGG COLOR Tinted or cream

EGG PRODUCTION Medium

SHOW CLASSIFICATION Light, Soft Feather

Yokohama

ROOSTER WEIGHT
Large Fowl 4–6 lb. (1.8–2.7 kg)
Bantam 20–24 oz. (570–680 g)

HEN WEIGHT
Large Fowl 2½–4 lb. (1.1–1.8 kg)
Bantam 16–20 oz. (490–570 g)

COUNTRY/REGION OF ORIGIN
Japan

Profile One of the most graceful and spectacular of chickens, the Yokohama is a long-tailed breed whose heritage receives government support in Japan. The breed has a horizontal carriage and the males have profuse tail feathering that can grow 3 feet 3 inches (1 m) a season in controlled conditions (in natural conditions this feathering will molt annually). Most commonly seen in the red-saddled variety, it makes a stunning entry on the show bench.

Behavior & upkeep The incredibly ornate appearance of the Yokohama belies its active nature; it needs a good amount of space to thrive. If kept for exhibition purposes, it requires dry, sheltered housing to keep its extensive tail feathers clean and in top condition. Perches should also be positioned high enough to let the tail feathering hang clear of the ground. The breed has some underlying game qualities that can make the roosters intolerant and aggressive toward their keeper, other breeds, and each other. Some find it easier to house rooster birds alone to avoid mess and feather pecking.

COLOR
Plumage White, red saddled, black/red, duckwing (gold and silver)
Eyes Red **Comb** Single, pea or walnut, small
Feet & legs Yellow, blue, or white (depending on plumage)

EGG COLOR Tinted

EGG PRODUCTION Low

SHOW CLASSIFICATION Light; Rare

Sumatra

ROOSTER WEIGHT
Large Fowl 5–6 lb. (2.25–2.7 kg)
Bantam 26 oz. (735 g)

HEN WEIGHT
Large Fowl 4–5 lb. (1.8–2.25 kg)
Bantam 22 oz. (625 g)

COUNTRY/REGION OF ORIGIN
Indonesia

Profile The Sumatra is literally a breed apart. It does not share its ancestry with other poultry, but descends from a now-extinct species of wild fowl. It has a game fowl look combined with profuse feathering and a distinctive green sheen to its black plumage. It is easily distinguishable by its long tail and pheasantlike carriage, which give the bird a regal air. It reached North America in the mid-nineteenth century and Europe a few decades later.

Behavior & upkeep This is a busy breed that needs a lot of space, both indoors and out, partly to avoid damage to its long tail feathers. The birds can be allowed to free roam but, given the choice, they will roost in trees as opposed to housing, so a roofed-in run is advisable. They are not a fast-growing breed and are slow to mature; they should be fed higher-protein feeds to promote the full development of their feathering. The roosters will show aggression toward each other, and birds or both sexes like to remain active, but they will become tame in response to calm handling.

COLOR
Plumage Black, blue **Eyes** Black
Comb Pea, small **Feet & legs** Featherless, black

EGG COLOR White
EGG PRODUCTION Medium
SHOW CLASSIFICATION Light; Rare

Cochin

ROOSTER WEIGHT
Large Fowl 10–13 lb. (4.55–5.9 kg)

HEN WEIGHT
Large Fowl 9–11 lb. (4.1–5 kg)

COUNTRY/REGION OF ORIGIN
China

Profile Originally known as the Shanghai, the Cochin reached the Western world from China in the 1850s. It was initially hailed for its mixture of table and egg-laying qualities, but focus has gradually shifted to its profuse plumage and exhibition potential. Its fluffy feathering, short feathered legs, and low carriage give it a markedly bulky appearance.

Behavior & upkeep The Cochin is as placid and soft as it looks. It is easy to tame and shows little desire to get off the ground. Its size means that it needs generously proportioned housing, and perches must not be set too high to enable the bird to alight without causing itself damage. Its feathering makes it less well able to cope in muddy conditions, so dry sheltered areas must be provided whether the birds are free roaming or kept in a fixed run. The hens are good layers and regularly turn broody, making reliable mothers.

COLOR Plumage Black, blue, buff, cuckoo, partridge, white (not shown: splash) **Eyes** Bright red, dark red, or pearl, depending on plumage type **Comb** Single, small, evenly serrated **Feet & legs** Feathered, color dependent on plumage type

EGG COLOR Tinted

EGG PRODUCTION Medium

SHOW CLASSIFICATION Heavy; Soft Feather

Brahma

ROOSTER WEIGHT
Large Fowl 10–12 lb. (4.5–5.5 kg)
Bantam 38 oz. (1.08kg)

HEN WEIGHT
Large Fowl 7–9 lb. (3.2–4.2 kg)
Bantam 32 oz. (910 g)

COUNTRY/REGION OF ORIGIN
North America

Profile A striking, heavy breed, the Brahma was created in North America and imported to Europe in 1852. Known as the "King Of Chickens," it is one of the largest breeds available and has played a major part in the creation of new breeds and colors. It has an upright stance, a broad deep body, and full feathering that extends onto the legs and feet. Coupled with the "beetle brow" seen in both sexes, this can give the breed a menacing look.

Behavior & upkeep Despite their appearance, Brahmas are gentle giants with a placid nature, which makes them an ideal starter chicken. Consideration must be given to their immense size; their accommodation, and access to and from it, must be proportionately bigger. They do not, however, need a larger space in which to roam; they are not known to wander far. They do not fly, so a low-fenced run with no roof will keep them contained. The feathering on their feet means that they are less prone to cause damage to a yard; however, they are not suited to muddy conditions.

COLOR
Plumage White, dark, light, gold partridge, blue partridge, black, blue Columbian, buff Columbian **Eyes** Orange to red
Comb Triple (pea) **Feet & legs** Yellow and feathered

EGG COLOR Cream

EGG PRODUCTION Medium to high

SHOW CLASSIFICATION Heavy; Soft Feather

Frizzle

ROOSTER WEIGHT
Large Fowl 8 lb. (3.6 kg)
Bantam 24–28 oz. (680–790 g)

HEN WEIGHT
Large Fowl 6 lb. (2.7 kg)
Bantam 20–24 oz. (570–680 g)

COUNTRY/REGION OF ORIGIN
Asia

Profile The Frizzle gets its name from its curled feathers, which bend away from the body. The genetic mutation that causes such feathering is also known to occur in other breeds, such as Japanese and Polands, but the Frizzle is recognized as a distinct breed. Its existence was first noted in the eighteenth century, with cases referred to in India, Java, and the Philippines. It is predominantly a show breed but it does have reasonable laying capability.

Behavior & upkeep As relatively calm birds, Frizzles can be tamed easily. Their distinctive feathering makes them less capable of flight, so a low fence can contain them. They are capable of coping in poor conditions, but it is a good idea to provide a sheltered area so that they can avoid the worst of the weather. They make good foragers and work well in a free-roaming environment. The hens lay a reasonable number of eggs and turn broody easily, making excellent mothers.

COLOR
Plumage Multiple **Eyes** Red **Comb** Single, medium
Feet & legs Featherless, color should be same as beak

EGG COLOR Tinted or white

EGG PRODUCTION Medium

SHOW CLASSIFICATION Heavy; Soft Feather

Appenzeller Spitzhauben

ROOSTER WEIGHT
Large Fowl 3½–4½ lb. (1.6–2 kg)

HEN WEIGHT
Large Fowl 3–3½ lb. (1.35–1.6 kg)

COUNTRY/REGION OF ORIGIN
Switzerland

Profile This is an old breed that can be traced back to the Swiss monasteries of the sixteenth century. It is, however, a relatively modern addition to the wider world of poultry, with exports to the United Kingdom, for example, only occurring during the early 1970s. In recent years, its alert bearing, distinctive forward-pointing crest, and good laying qualities have seen it gain a growing and enthusiastic following.

Behavior & upkeep Despite its light ornamental appearance, this breed is surprisingly active and hardy. It forages well and is tolerant of poor weather conditions. Its country fowl background makes it a good flyer with a wary character; it needs suitably high fencing or a roofed-in run and will only become hand tame if treated with great patience. It will happily live within a mixed flock, but care must be taken to make sure the crest is not subjected to the feather-pecking attentions of other breeds. The hens lay a good number of eggs and are not prone to broodiness.

COLOR
Plumage Black, silver spangled, gold spangled **Eyes** Dark brown
Comb Horn, spiked **Feet & legs** Featherless, blue

EGG COLOR White

EGG PRODUCTION Medium to high

SHOW CLASSIFICATION Light; Soft Feather

Transylvanian Naked Neck

ROOSTER WEIGHT
Large Fowl 7–8 lb. (3.2–3.6 kg)
Bantam 32 oz. (910 g)

HEN WEIGHT
Large Fowl 5½–6½ lb. (2.5–2.7 kg)
Bantam 24 oz. (680 g)

COUNTRY/REGION OF ORIGIN
Eastern Europe

Profile This striking breed gets its name from the lack of feathers on its neck. It is a characteristic that divides opinion. Some love the breed for its unusual appearance; others find it unappealing. Chickens with naked necks are found in many regions of the world, but today's standard Transylvanian breed was developed from birds from eastern Hungary. The same defining feature is being exploited in the development of broiler breeds for warmer countries.

Behavior & upkeep Despite a somewhat vulnerable appearance, this is a hardy and vigorous breed that thrives in any weather conditions. The birds are relatively heavy and not inclined to fly, and can be kept in a run or free roaming. If allowed to roam, they forage intensively and take little of the food supplied by the keeper. Their temperament is calm and easy to tame. The hens lay in reasonable quantities and can easily become broody, although their tight feathering restricts their hatching ability and they are not able to sit on many eggs.

COLOR
Plumage Black, white, blue, red, buff, cuckoo **Eyes** Orange
Comb Single, even spikes **Feet & legs** Featherless, yellow, horn, or white, depending on plumage

EGG COLOR Tinted

EGG PRODUCTION Medium

SHOW CLASSIFICATION Heavy; Rare

Sultan

ROOSTER WEIGHT
Large Fowl 6 lb. (2.7 kg)
Bantam 24–28 oz. (680–790 g)

HEN WEIGHT
Large Fowl 4½ lb. (2 kg)
Bantam 18–24 oz. (510–680 g)

COUNTRY/REGION OF ORIGIN
Turkey

Profile Tradition has it that this highly ornamental breed could once be found roaming the palace gardens of the Sultan of Constantinople. Records state that the specimens seen today descend from a crate of original palace birds imported by a Miss Elizabeth Watts of Hampstead in the United Kingdom in 1854. The Sultan is an exotic breed sporting a head crest, beard, horned comb, and pale blue, feathered legs. It has a deep, neat, low-slung stature and the males carry a longish, upright tail.

Behavior & upkeep The Sultan is not a breed often encountered, but its owners are usually enthused by its docility and proud appearance. Described as "pearls among fowl," they require additional care to keep their profuse feathering in good condition. They need clean, dry, roofed-in runs, and drinkers and feeders should preferably be located at beak level so that their beards and crests do not become wet or soiled. The hens are reasonable layers but are not known for broodiness—although this should not be discounted.

COLOR
Plumage White **Eyes** Red **Comb** Two-spiked horn
Feet & legs Profuse feathering, five toes, white or pale blue

EGG COLOR White

EGG PRODUCTION Medium

SHOW CLASSIFICATION Light; Rare

True Bantam 〜

HISTORY

"Bantam" is a catch-all term applied to any small or diminutive chicken. True Bantams, however, are a group apart from other breeds of chicken. They are miniature by definition and have no large-fowl counterpart.

Their name is taken from the Banten Province in Indonesia, where European sailors first came across these breeds of small chicken. The birds were brought to the West during the early sixteenth century and made a significant contribution toward the evolution and development of additional breeds, as well as the "bantamizing" of some large-fowl breeds.

Despite the origins of their name, it is believed that these tiny birds did not originally hail from Indonesia but from China and Japan, where such breed types still have an enthusiastic following.

CHARACTERISTICS

True Bantams tend to be ornamental birds and have a "showy" character, so it is safe to say that these birds belong more in the exhibition scene than as part of the household economy. In this respect, true Bantams differ from those bantams that are simply a miniaturized version of a large-fowl breed. These latter types of bantam tend to exhibit characteristics similar to their larger cousins, although many breeders would say they show a little more "attitude" toward the keeper.

This is possibly brought about by the focus on breeding primarily for size—to the neglect of temperament. Because the true Bantams have no large-fowl counterpart, the disposition of the breed group is better defined. They usually have a proud stature and easily become used to being handled.

A number of breeds in this group show a propensity toward turning broody and make excellent mothers, with the roosters often helping in the rearing of the young. They are not known for their egg-laying qualities but, given the right conditions, they will provide a reasonably steady supply.

Below *The intricate lacing of the Sebright appears as if it has been carefully painted on the plumage.*

CARE & MANAGEMENT

Due to their size, Bantam fowl can be kept in a much smaller space than large fowl and they can make an excellent choice for the average backyard. Many of the breeds are perfect for children, too, ideally suited for small hands, and if a docile breed is selected, they can make superb pets and a great introduction to chicken keeping. Their henhouse, feeding stations, and drinkers can also be smaller, which, in turn, can make for a more affordable hobby.

Accommodation

Attention, however, should be paid to the perches and nest boxes within the house, because these need to be reduced in size if the birds are to be comfortable. The more flighty breeds will need a roofed-in run because they are capable of taking to the wing and reaching the uppermost branches of a tree.

Ground conditions

The diminutive stature of Bantams means that ground conditions need to be managed slightly differently. Certain breeds, such as the Japanese Bantams, with their short legs, can soon see their breast feathers fouled in wet conditions, and muddy ground will quickly mat the feathering of feather-footed varieties, such as the Booted Bantam. As far as possible, the ground should be kept dry.

Japanese

ROOSTER WEIGHT
18–20 oz. (510–600 g)

HEN WEIGHT
14–18 oz. (400–510 g)

COUNTRY/REGION OF ORIGIN
Japan

Profile The Japanese Bantam, occasionally known as the Chabo, is an ancient breed. The original birds hailed from China, but it was in Japan that the bird gained popularity and was bred to its current standard. These tiny birds were first seen in Europe around the sixteenth century and are the shortest-legged of all the breeds. They are low slung and broad in stature, with upright tails and proud breasts giving them a showy character. They come in three different plumage types.

Behavior & upkeep Their short legs give Japanese Bantams a shuffling gait, and they need to be provided with a well-maintained and dry run if they are to look their best. They are ideal chickens for children because of their placid and trusting nature. The rooster birds can be particularly striking in their shape and character and will add to the overall attractiveness of any flock. They have a relatively soft crow, which they use infrequently compared to other breeds of chicken. The hens are not prolific layers and their eggs are tiny.

COLOR Plumage Black-tailed white, black-tailed buff, Columbian, white, black, grays, black/red, red, blues (not shown: mottled, cuckoo) **Eyes** Color dependent on color of plumage **Comb** Single, large **Feet & legs** Short, featherless, color dependent on plumage

EGG COLOR Cream

EGG PRODUCTION Low

SHOW CLASSIFICATION True Bantam

Belgian Barbu d'Anvers

ROOSTER WEIGHT
Bantam 24–28 oz. (680–790 g)

HEN WEIGHT
Bantam 20–24 oz. (570–680 g)

COUNTRY/REGION OF ORIGIN
Belgium

Profile The Barbu d'Anvers is also known as the "Bearded Antwerp," thanks to its fully feathered throat area. It is one of the oldest true Bantams in Europe, with the quail-type female first recorded in a seventh-century painting. The breed appears in a vast array of colors, with the appearance of its plumage figuring highly in the exhibition points system; it is a popular fixture at Bantam shows. The cocks are often seen without spurs, and breeders prefer small combs and wattles.

Behavior & upkeep Barbu d'Anvers are active little birds, but cope quite well living in a small run. Their drinkers should be small and positioned at head level to reduce beard soiling. They have a friendly nature and can be quick to become tame if handled calmly. The hens can be tolerant of each other, but the rooster birds can become aggressive toward the keeper during the breeding season. The roosters are also noteworthy for their high-pitched, shrill crow. The hens can turn broody, but this is not a dominant feature in the breed.

 COLOR Plumage Multiple, including black, blue, buff, mottled, cuckoo, porcelain, white, Columbian, buff Columbian (not shown: millefleur, quail, blue quail) **Eyes** Dark, color depends on plumage **Comb** Rose **Feet & legs** Featherless, color depends on plumage

EGG COLOR Tinted

EGG PRODUCTION Medium

SHOW CLASSIFICATION True Bantam; Rare

Dutch

ROOSTER WEIGHT
Bantam 18–20 oz. (500–550 g)

HEN WEIGHT
Bantam 14–16 oz. (400–450 g)

COUNTRY/REGION OF ORIGIN
Netherlands

Profile The Dutch was not formally recognized in its home country until the early twentieth century, but it is actually an old breed. It is one of the smallest breeds of chicken and among the most attractive to own and exhibit, and it is popular worldwide for its huge variety of plumage colors, jaunty posture, and slight build.

Behavior & upkeep Although the Dutch is an active breed, its size means it can be kept in a relatively small space, making it ideal for the smaller yard. They need no special care other than to be kept in a draft-free house to protect them from the worst of the elements. They are tolerant of each other and can be easily tamed; qualities that make them highly suitable for young children. The hens lay a reasonable number of eggs, although these are small. They can also turn broody and make excellent mothers to their tiny offspring.

COLOR Plumage Multiple, including but not limited to black, white, blue, lavender, black/red, blue/red, cuckoo, duckwing (silver, gold, blue/yellow, blue/silver), pyle **Eyes** Orange, red **Comb** Single, five serrations **Feet & legs** Featherless, slate blue or white

EGG COLOR Tinted

EGG PRODUCTION Medium

SHOW CLASSIFICATION True Bantam

Nankin

ROOSTER WEIGHT
24–26 oz. (680–735 g)

HEN WEIGHT
20–22 oz. (570–620 g)

COUNTRY/REGION OF ORIGIN
Asia

Profile A handsome and sprightly little bird, the Nankin was once one of the most widespread true Bantams. Recent years have seen it decline in numbers and it is now considered rare. This may be because it only comes in one color—a rich buff. Some say its color resembles that of the Chinese nankeen cloth, which may explain the origin of the breed's name.

Behavior & upkeep The Nankin is a hardy little breed and easy to keep, with no special requirements beyond that of other Bantams. It has a trusting nature and with correct handling can become tame. The hens will lay a reasonable number of eggs but tend to stop laying during the winter months. They can turn broody—a characteristic that once made them popular among gamekeepers for hatching game birds—and will make good mothers. They are nonaggressive and tolerant of other breeds, which means they can easily be incorporated within a mixed Bantam flock. They are ideal for the smaller yard.

COLOR
Plumage Buff **Eyes** Orange
Comb Single or rose **Feet & legs** Featherless, blue, or slate

EGG COLOR Tinted

EGG PRODUCTION Medium

SHOW CLASSIFICATION True Bantam; Rare

Booted Bantam

ROOSTER WEIGHT
Bantam 30 oz. (850 g)

HEN WEIGHT
Bantam 27 oz. (750 g)

COUNTRY/REGION OF ORIGIN
Europe

Profile The Booted Bantam, also known as the Sabelpoot, is an ancient European Bantam breed with origins in Italy, Germany, the Netherlands, and Britain. They are proud and beautiful birds with a friendly, jaunty personality. In build, they are short and stocky, but an upright stance makes them look slender. The term "booted" refers to the long, stiff leg hocks, or "sabels," which can be seen on both males and females.

Behavior & upkeep Despite its size, the Booted Bantam is hardy and makes a good bird for beginners or a small yard. Their feathered feet mean limited damage to the yard if you let them roam freely, but they are not suitable for muddy conditions. Inquisitive by nature, they seem to seek out the company of their keepers, resulting in them becoming reasonably tame. The hens lay a good number of decently sized eggs, 1½ ounces (38 g), and occasionally become broody. The rooster birds are fairly tolerant and not prone to aggressive behavior. They also have a relatively quiet crow compared to other breeds.

COLOR
Plumage Black, white, porcelain, black mottled (not shown: millefleur) **Eyes** Red, dark red, dark brown **Comb** Single, upright, well serrated **Feet & legs** Well feathered; white

EGG COLOR Tinted

EGG PRODUCTION Medium

SHOW CLASSIFICATION True Bantam; Rare

Sebright

ROOSTER WEIGHT
Bantam 22 oz. (620 g)

HEN WEIGHT
Bantam 18 oz. (510 g)

COUNTRY/REGION OF ORIGIN
United Kingdom

Profile The Sebright is a truly ornamental breed and it has a long history, being one of the oldest genuine Bantam breeds in its native home of Great Britain. It was created around 1800 by landowner Sir John Sebright, although it is uncertain which breeds he used. The Sebright's plumage is remarkably laced and it has an attractively jaunty appearance. It is a stunning bird to keep, especially for those interested in the exhibition scene.

Behavior & upkeep This breed tames easily and can be kept within a small run. The male's crow is neither loud nor shrill, which with careful management can make it a suitable breed for the urban environment. The hens are poor layers and can occasionally turn broody. However, the males tend to be active only during the warm spring months, which makes successful breeding more of a challenge for the keeper. They can cope with poor weather but are better suited to a milder climate and can benefit from overwintering indoors. Sebrights are highly susceptible to Marek's disease; vaccinated stock should be sought when purchasing.

COLOR
Plumage Gold, silver **Eyes** Black
Comb Rose, dull red **Feet & legs** Featherless, slate blue

EGG COLOR Cream or white

EGG PRODUCTION Low

SHOW CLASSIFICATION True Bantam

The Evolution of
Commercial Strains ∼

The fancy fowl frenzy of the mid-nineteenth century brought with it the realization that chickens could be carefully bred and reared instead of simply allowed to forage around the farmyard. This breeding trend began as a quest for aesthetic appeal and prestige among wealthy landowners, but over the course of the next one hundred years, the same principles were increasingly applied to productivity—both in terms of eggs and meat. The two world wars in the first half of the twentieth century accelerated the process; demand for meat was high and supply was low. Could chickens become an economical source of cheap protein?

Below *Chickens are seen as a valuable alternative source of protein by the meat industry.*

Above *Consistent high-volume laying performance is an essential quality in commercial laying strains.*

This was the question at the heart of the "Chicken-Of-Tomorrow Contest" launched across the United States in the austere years immediately following World War II. Organized by farmers, breeders, and suppliers, and backed by cash prizes from A&P grocery stores, the contest invited chicken breeders to "create" the ultimate breed of meat chicken; that is, the one that provided the most meat in the shortest time and for the lowest feed cost. It marked a step change in the history of poultry—from "farm chicken" to "chicken farming." In no time at all, poultry became an alternative source of protein across the world.

Breeding for commercial hybrids

As the industry boomed, breeding programs became more and more scientific. Biologists and geneticists helped to refine the process of crossbreeding so that new hybrids could be created. It became possible to pursue two discrete breeding programs, one for egg-laying "machines" and another for fast-growing table birds. It was also discovered that careful manipulation of environmental conditions could cause birds to perform beyond the levels they would reach in more natural circumstances.

Hybrids were produced that, given the right conditions, were capable of laying more than 300 eggs in the first year of lay, and others that could reach a suitable size for the table within eight weeks of hatching, a feat no heritage breed could ever achieve. With modern commercial strains and husbandry practices, output has become the key. Meat and eggs—instead of chickens—are the products farmed.

Commercial versus heritage breeeds

Science and agriculture continue to work hand in hand with suppliers to meet the ever-increasing demand for poultry-based products. It has reached the stage where it no longer makes much sense to use breed names when referring to these commercial chickens; their titles are more akin to the make and model of a motor vehicle, with heritage breeds now the preserve of the hobbyist.

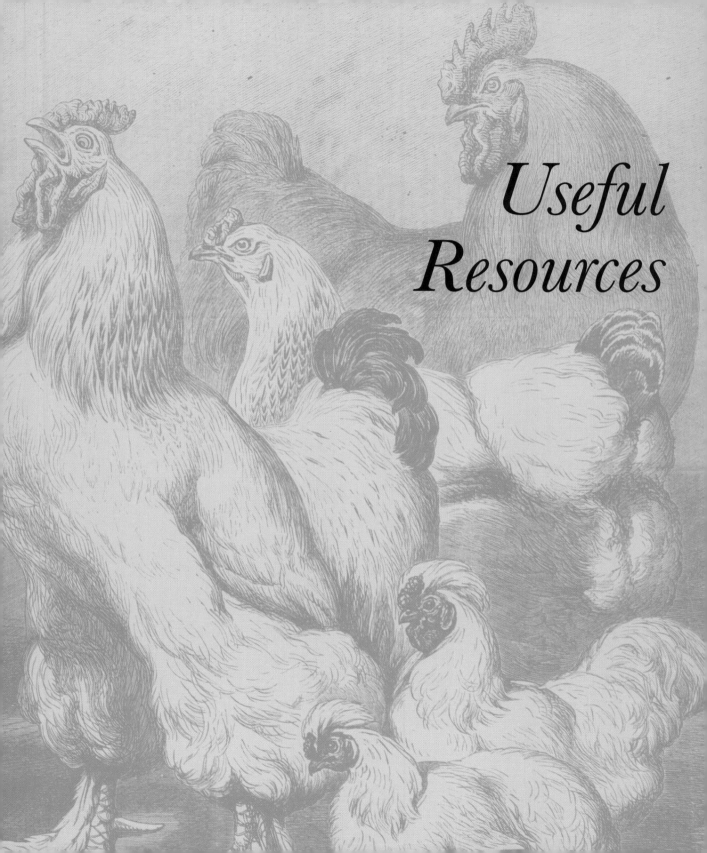

Useful
Resources

Breeds List

DUAL-PURPOSE BREEDS

Amrock
Augsburger
Basque
Bielefelder
Bresse
California Gray
Catalana
Chantecler
Croad Langshan
Delaware
Dominique
Famenne
Groninger Meeuwen
Ixworth
La Flèche

Mantes
Marsh Daisy
Norfolk Grey
Old English Pheasant Fowl
Orloff
Penedesenca
Polverara
Redcap
Reichshuhner
Scots Dumpy
Shumenska
Sulmtaler
Sussex
Vorwerk

GAME BREEDS

American Game Fowl
Aseel
Australian Pit Fowl
Bruges
Ga Noi Game Fowl
Indian Game (Cornish)
Ko Shamo
Malay
Modern Game

Nankin-Shamo
Old English Game
Raiza
Rumpless Game
Satsumadori
Shamo
Totenko
Yamato-Gunkei

LAYER BREEDS

Ancona
Andalusian
Arauncana
Ardenner
Australorp
Barnevelder
Bassette
Brabanconne
Brakel
Campine
Castilian
Drenthe fowl
Dresdener
Du Mans
Fayoumi
Friesian
Green-legged Partridge
   Fowl
Hamburgh
Icelandic fowl
Italiener
Lakenvelder
Legbar

Leghorn
Lincolnshire Buff
Marans
Minorca
New Hampshire Red
Norwegian Jærhøns
Orpington
Ovambo
Plymouth Rock
Rheinlander
Rhode Island
Rhodebar
Saxon
Scots Gray
Sicilian Buttercup
Swedish Spotted
Twentse Fowl
Welbar
Welsummer
Westfalische Totleger
Wyandotte
Wybar

MEAT BREEDS

Altsteirer	*Faverolles*
Breda Fowl	*Houdan*
Buckeye	*Java*
Coucou de Rennes	*Jersey Giant*
Crevecoeur	*Maline*
Dorking	*Niederrhein Fowl*
Estaires	*North Holland Blue*

ORNAMENTAL BREEDS

Appenzeller Barthuhner	*Owl Beard*
Appenzeller Spitzhauben	*Poland*
Brabanter	*Red Junglefowl*
Brahma	*Silkie*
Cochin	*Sultan*
Denizli	*Sumatra*
Frizzle	*Thuringian*
German Langshan	*Transylvanian Naked Neck*
Koeyoshi	*Venda*
Modern Langshan	*White-Faced Black Spanish*
Ogye	*Yokohama*

TRUE BANTAM BREEDS

Belgian de Watermaal	*Dutch*
Belgian d'Uccle	*Fantail Ma Lai*
Belgium Barbu d'Anvers	*Japanese*
Booted Bantam (Sabelpoot)	*Nankin*
Burmese	*Sebright*

Author Biographies

CHAPTER 1 *Evolution & Domestication*
by Janet Daly

Janet Daly is a lecturer in comparative virology, Faculty of Medicine & Health Sciences, School of Veterinary Medicine and Science, University of Nottingham. She has a BSc (Hons) in animal physiology and nutrition from the University of Leeds.

CHAPTER 2 *Anatomy & Biology*
by Catrin Rutland

Catrin Rutland is a lecturer in anatomy and developmental genetics, Faculty of Medicine & Health Sciences, School of Veterinary Medicine and Science, University of Nottingham. She has a BSc (Hons) in applied biology and completed her PhD at the University of Nottingham.

CHAPTER 3 *Behavior*
by Dr Mark Hauber

Dr Mark Hauber works in the Department of Psychology, Hunter College and the Graduate Center of the City University of New York, where he is professor in animal behavior and conservation and head of biopsychology and behavioral neuroscience. He has a PhD from Cornell University in neurobiology and behavior, is editor of *Ethology* and former editor of *Behavioral Ecology*, and his research has been funded by HFSP, NIH, NSF, and the National Geographic Society.

CHAPTER 4 *Intelligence & Learning*
by Dr Joseph Barber

Dr Joseph Barber is co-editor of the *Journal of Applied Animal Welfare Science* (JAAWS), adjunct assistant professor at Hunter College of the City University of New York and associate director at the University of Pennsylvania. He specializes in scientific presentations accessible to the general public, animal welfare science and science writing.

CHAPTER 5 *Breeds*
by Andy Cawthray

Andy Cawthray has a degree in ecology and conservation, and has worked for the Field Studies Council and the Royal Society for the Protection of Birds (RSPB). He writes for a number of magazines and newspapers on chicken husbandry and breeds. He also provides talks and courses on keeping poultry at home.

Bibliography

BOOKS

Beeken L (2010) *Haynes Chicken Manual: The Complete Step-by-Step Guide to Keeping Chickens.* J.H. Haynes & Co. Ltd. ISBN: 1844257290.

Frandson RD, Wilke WL and Fails AD (2009) *Anatomy and Physiology of Farm Animals.* 7th Edition. John Wiley & Sons Ltd. UK.

Hayhurst J (1947) *The Small Poultry Farm.* Pearson Ltd.

Kay, I (1997) *Stairway to the Breeds.* Scribblers Publishing Ltd.

Roberts V (ed.) (1997) *British Poultry Standards.* 5th Edition. Blackwell Science.

Scrivener D (2005) *Exhibition Poultry Keeping.* The Crowood Press.

Squier SM (2011) *Poultry Science, Chicken Culture: A Partial Alphabet.* Rutgers University Press.

Verhoff E, Rijs A (2003) *The Complete Encyclopaedia of Chickens.* Rebo Publishers.

Webster J (2011) *Management and Welfare of Farm Animals: UFAW Farm Handbook.* 5th Edition. John Wiley & Sons Ltd. UK.

Willis K, Ludlow R (2009) *Raising Chickens for Dummies.* ISBN: 0470465441.

MAGAZINES

Country Smallholding – Archant Publishing www.countrysmallholding.com

Fancy Fowl – Today Magazines Ltd www.fancyfowl.com

Poultry World – from *Farmers Weekly* www.fwi.co.uk

World's Poultry Science Journal – The World's Poultry Science Association (WPSA) journals.cambridge.org

JOURNALS

Bateman AJ (1948) Intra-sexual selection in Drosophila. *Journal of Heredity* 2, 349–368.

Brawn TP, Nusbaum HC, Margoliash D (2010) Sleep-dependent consolidation of auditory discrimination learning in adult starlings. *The Journal of Neuroscience* 30, 609–613.

Burt DW (2005) Chicken genome: Current status and future opportunities. *Genome Research* 15, 1692–1698.

Chiandetti C, Vallortigara G (2011) Chicks like consonant music. *Psychological Science* 22, 1270–1273.

Evans CS, Evans L (1998) Chicken food calls are functionally referential. *Animal Behaviour* 58, 307–319.

Hishikawa Y, Cramer H, and Kuhlo W (1969) Natural and melatonin-induced sleep in young chickens: A behavioral and electrographic study. *Experimental Brain Research* 7, 84–94.

Honza M, Picman J, Grim T, Novák V, Capek Jr, M, and Mrlík V (2001) How to hatch from an egg of great structural strength: A study of the common cuckoo. *Journal of Avian Biology* 32, 249–255.

Karakashian SJ, Gyger M, and Marler P (1988) Audience effects on alarm calling in chickens (*Gallus gallus*). *Journal of Comparative Psychology* 102, 129–135.

Krakauer AH (2005) Kin selection and cooperative courtship in wild turkeys. *Nature* 434, 69–72.

Nicol CJ (1996) Farm animal cognition. *Animal Science* 62, 375–391.

Pizzari T, Birkhead T (2000) Female feral fowl eject sperm of subdominant males. *Nature* 405, 787–789.

Pizzari T, Cornwallis CK, and Froman DP (2007) Social competitiveness associated with rapid fluctuations in sperm quality in domestic fowl. *Proceedings of the Royal Society of London* B74, 853–860.

Rugani R, Fontanari L, Simoni E, Regolin L, and Vallortigara G (2009) Arithmetic in newborn chicks. *Proceedings of the Royal Society of Biological Sciences* 276, 2451–2460.

Seyfarth RM, Cheney DL, and Marler P (1980) Monkey responses to three different alarm calls: evidence of predator classification and semantic communication. *Science* 210, 801–803.

Taylor PE, Haskell M, Appleby MC, and Waran NK (2002) Perception of time duration by domestic hens. *Applied Animal Behaviour Science* 76, 41–51.

WEBSITES

Backyard Chickens
www.backyardchickens.com

Feathersite
www.feathersite.com

The Poultry Keeper
poultrykeeper.com

The Poultry Site
www.thepoultrysite.com

World Poultry
www.worldpoultry.net

Index ～

Acknowledgments

AKG Images/Interfoto: 16B; Erich Lessing: 16T.

Alamy/19th era 2: 212; The Art Archive: 157; John Blair: 57; John Cairns: 137; Jose Elias/Lusoimages – Animals: 84; F1online digitale Bildagentur GmbH: 110; Juniors Bildarchiv: 99; Kim Karpeles: 148; The Natural History Museum: 15; David Page: 149; PetStockBoys: 142.

Andy Cawthray/ChickenStreet.co.uk: 154.

Corbis: 115; Alan Bailey/Rubberball: 119T; Nigel Cattlin/Visuals Unlimited: 131; Robert Dowling: 27, 47, 189; Lowell Georgia: 92; Sven Hagolani: 18; Jakob Helbig/cultura: 79; Helmut Meyer zur Capellen: 5; Ocean: 109, 211; Robert Pickett: 119B.

Janet Daly & Catrin Rutland: 26, 33, 41B, 42R.

Tim Daniels & Rupert Stephenson/poultrykeeper.com: 162, 163, 188, 200.

FLPA/Angela Hampton: 171; David Hosking: 42TL; Wayne Hutchinson: 69; Heidi & Hans-Jurgen Koch/Minden Pictures: 147; Gerard Lacz: 93, 184; Erica Olsen: 159, 170, 210; Picani/Imagebroker: 85; Gary K Smith: 203; David Tipling: 74.

My Pet Chicken/www.mypetchicken.com: 201.

Fotolia/Kryuchkov Alexey: 49; Anatolii: 95; Anistidesign: 105; Boric: 88; M.Camerin: 151; Chillingworths: 123; Kevin Eaves: 8; Fotomaster: 89; Adrian Hillman: 107; Eric Isselée: 22, 102, 191; Illarionovdv: 135; John1179: 103; Kneiane: 67; Lightpoet: 62; Lilya: 75; Living2Ride Photos: 117; Catherine Murray: 31; Martin Nemec: 132; Percent: 111; Pwollinga: 82; Rdnzl: 41T; Tomas Sereda: 48; Shiffti: 52; Snaptitude: 83; Sokratas: 44; TSpider: 91, 127; Wouter Tolenaars: 125; Velvetocean: 152; Wild Geese: 64; Jason Young: 86.

Getty Images/De Agostini: 17; Imagenavi: 77; Ineke Kamps: 7; National Geographic: 21; Grove Pashley: 19, 90; Ben Queenborough: 129.

Nature Picture Library/John Cancalosi: 58; Georgette Douwma: 73; Tony Heald: 130; Reinhard/ARCO: 65.

Photocase/Kimako: 11, 120.

Rex Features/Sipa Press: 20.

Science Photo Library: Eye of Science: 38; Edward Kinsman: 96, 97; David Scharf: 39.

Shutterstock: 112; Bogdanhoda: 28; Cameilia: 138; Tony Campbell: 140; Gosphotodesign: 9; Jocic: 63; M.Khebra: 81; Krugloff: 153; Lepas: 55; Guy J. Sagi: 71; Tomas Sereda: 145; Studio online: 42BL; TSpider: 100; Michael Woodruff: 51.